The Image of the City

Kevin Lynch

The Image of the City

The MIT Press

Massachusetts Institute of Technology
Cambridge, Massachusetts, and London, England

PUBLICATION OF THE JOINT CENTER FOR URBAN STUDIES

This book is one of a series published under the auspices of the Joint Center for Urban Studies, a cooperative venture of the Massachusetts Institute of Technology and Harvard University. The Joint Center was founded in 1959 to organize and encourage research on urban and regional problems.

Participants have included scholars from the fields of anthropology, architecture, business, city planning, economics, education, engineering, history, law, philosophy, political science, and sociology.

The findings and conclusions of this book are, as with all Joint Center publications, solely the responsibility of the author.

ISBN-13 978 0 262 12004 3 (hardcover)
ISBN-13 978 0 262 62001 7 (paperback)

ISBN 0 262 12004 6 (hardcover)
ISBN 0 262 62001 4 (paperback)

Library of Congress Catalog Card No: 60-7362
Printed in the United States of America

40 39 38 37 36 35

PREFACE

This book is about the look of cities, and whether this look is of any importance, and whether it can be changed. The urban landscape, among its many roles, is also something to be seen, to be remembered, and to delight in. Giving visual form to the city is a special kind of design problem, and a rather new one at that.

In the course of examining this new problem, the book looks at three American cities: Boston, Jersey City, and Los Angeles. It suggests a method whereby we might begin to deal with visual form at the urban scale, and offers some first principles of city design.

The work that lies behind this study was done under the direction of Professor Gyorgy Kepes and myself at the Center for Urban and Regional Studies of the Massachusetts Institute of Technology. It was generously supported over several years by funds from the Rockefeller Foundation. The book itself is being published as one of a series of volumes of the Joint Center for Urban Studies of the Massachusetts Institute of Technology and Harvard University, an agency which has grown out of the urban research activities of these two institutions.

As in any intellectual work, the content derives from many sources, difficult to trace. Several research associates contributed directly to the development of this study: David Crane, Bernard

Frieden, William Alonso, Frank Hotchkiss, Richard Dober, Mary Ellen Peters (now Mrs. Alonso). I am very grateful to them all.

One name should be on the title page with my own, if only he would thereby not be made responsible for the shortcomings of the book. That name is Gyorgy Kepes. The detailed development and concrete studies are my own, but the underlying concepts were generated in many exchanges with Professor Kepes. I would be at a loss to disentangle my ideas from his. For me these have been good years of association.

Kevin Lynch

M.I.T.
December, 1959

CONTENTS

I.

THE IMAGE OF THE ENVIRONMENT

Looking at cities can give a special pleasure, however commonplace the sight may be. Like a piece of architecture, the city is a construction in space, but one of vast scale, a thing perceived only in the course of long spans of time. City design is therefore a temporal art, but it can rarely use the controlled and limited sequences of other temporal arts like music. On different occasions and for different people, the sequences are reversed, interrupted, abandoned, cut across. It is seen in all lights and all weathers.

At every instant, there is more than the eye can see, more than the ear can hear, a setting or a view waiting to be explored. Nothing is experienced by itself, but always in relation to its surroundings, the sequences of events leading up to it, the memory of past experiences. Washington Street set in a farmer's field might look like the shopping street in the heart of Boston, and yet it would seem utterly different. Every citizen has had long associations with some part of his city, and his image is soaked in memories and meanings.

Moving elements in a city, and in particular the people and their activities, are as important as the stationary physical parts. We are not simply observers of this spectacle, but are ourselves a part of it, on the stage with the other participants. Most often, our perception of the city is not sustained, but rather partial, fragmentary, mixed with other concerns. Nearly every sense is in operation, and the image is the composite of them all.

Not only is the city an object which is perceived (and perhaps enjoyed) by millions of people of widely diverse class and character, but it is the product of many builders who are constantly modifying the structure for reasons of their own. While it may be stable in general outlines for some time, it is ever changing in detail. Only partial control can be exercised over its growth and form. There is no final result, only a continuous succession of phases. No wonder, then, that the art of shaping cities for sensuous enjoyment is an art quite separate from architecture or music or literature. It may learn a great deal from these other arts, but it cannot imitate them.

A beautiful and delightful city environment is an oddity, some would say an impossibility. Not one American city larger than a village is of consistently fine quality, although a few towns have some pleasant fragments. It is hardly surprising, then, that most Americans have little idea of what it can mean to live in such an environment. They are clear enough about the ugliness of the world they live in, and they are quite vocal about the dirt, the smoke, the heat, and the congestion, the chaos and yet the monotony of it. But they are hardly aware of the potential value of harmonious surroundings, a world which they may have briefly glimpsed only as tourists or as escaped vacationers. They can have little sense of what a setting can mean in terms of daily delight, or as a continuous anchor for their lives, or as an extension of the meaningfulness and richness of the world.

Legibility

This book will consider the visual quality of the American city by studying the mental image of that city which is held by its citizens. It will concentrate especially on one particular visual quality: the apparent clarity or "legibility" of the cityscape. By this we mean the ease with which its parts can be recognized and can be organized into a coherent pattern. Just as this printed page, if it is legible, can be visually grasped as a related pattern of recognizable symbols, so a legible city would be one whose districts or landmarks or pathways are easily identifiable and are easily grouped into an over-all pattern.

This book will assert that legibility is crucial in the city setting, will analyze it in some detail, and will try to show how this concept might be used today in rebuilding our cities. As will quickly become apparent to the reader, this study is a preliminary exploration, a first word not a last word, an attempt to capture ideas and to suggest how they might be developed and tested. Its tone will be speculative and perhaps a little irresponsible: at once tentative and presumptuous. This first chapter will develop some of the basic ideas; later chapters will apply them to several American cities and discuss their consequences for urban design.

Although clarity or legibility is by no means the only important property of a beautiful city, it is of special importance when considering environments at the urban scale of size, time, and complexity. To understand this, we must consider not just the city as a thing in itself, but the city being perceived by its inhabitants.

Structuring and identifying the environment is a vital ability among all mobile animals. Many kinds of cues are used: the visual sensations of color, shape, motion, or polarization of light, as well as other senses such as smell, sound, touch, kinesthesia, sense of gravity, and perhaps of electric or magnetic fields. These techniques of orientation, from the polar flight of a tern to the path-finding of a limpet over the micro-topography of a rock, are described and their importance underscored in an extensive literature.[10, 20, 31, 59] Psychologists have also studied this ability in man, although rather sketchily or under limited laboratory conditions.[1, 5, 8, 12, 37, 63, 65, 76, 81] Despite a few remaining puzzles, it now seems unlikely that there is any mystic "instinct" of way-finding. Rather there is a consistent use and organization of definite sensory cues from the external environment. This organization is fundamental to the efficiency and to the very survival of free-moving life.

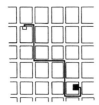

To become completely lost is perhaps a rather rare experience for most people in the modern city. We are supported by the presence of others and by special way-finding devices: maps, street numbers, route signs, bus placards. But let the mishap of disorientation once occur, and the sense of anxiety and even terror that accompanies it reveals to us how closely it is linked to our sense of balance and well-being. The very word "lost" in our language means much more than simple geographical uncertainty; it carries overtones of utter disaster.

In the process of way-finding, the strategic link is the environmental image, the generalized mental picture of the exterior physical world that is held by an individual. This image is the product both of immediate sensation and of the memory of past experience, and it is used to interpret information and to guide action. The need to recognize and pattern our surroundings is so crucial, and has such long roots in the past, that this image has wide practical and emotional importance to the individual.

Obviously a clear image enables one to move about easily and quickly: to find a friend's house or a policeman or a button store. But an ordered environment can do more than this; it may serve as a broad frame of reference, an organizer of activity or belief or knowledge. On the basis of a structural understanding of Manhattan, for example, one can order a substantial quantity of facts and fancies about the nature of the world we live in. Like any good framework, such a structure gives the individual a possibility of choice and a starting-point for the acquisition of further information. A clear image of the surroundings is thus a useful basis for individual growth.

A vivid and integrated physical setting, capable of producing a sharp image, plays a social role as well. It can furnish the raw material for the symbols and collective memories of group communication. A striking landscape is the skeleton upon which many primitive races erect their socially important myths. Common memories of the "home town" were often the first and easiest point of contact between lonely soldiers during the war.

A good environmental image gives its possessor an important sense of emotional security. He can establish an harmonious relationship between himself and the outside world. This is the obverse of the fear that comes with disorientation; it means that the sweet sense of home is strongest when home is not only familiar but distinctive as well.

Indeed, a distinctive and legible environment not only offers security but also heightens the potential depth and intensity of human experience. Although life is far from impossible in the visual chaos of the modern city, the same daily action could take on new meaning if carried out in a more vivid setting. Potentially, the city is in itself the powerful symbol of a complex society. If visually well set forth, it can also have strong expressive meaning.

It may be argued against the importance of physical legibility that the human brain is marvelously adaptable, that with some experience one can learn to pick one's way through the most disordered or featureless surroundings. There are abundant examples of precise navigation over the "trackless" wastes of sea, sand, or ice, or through a tangled maze of jungle.

See Appendix A

Yet even the sea has the sun and stars, the winds, currents, birds, and sea-colors without which unaided navigation would be impossible. The fact that only skilled professionals could navigate among the Polynesian Islands, and this only after extensive training, indicates the difficulties imposed by this particular environment. Strain and anxiety accompanied even the best-prepared expeditions.

In our own world, we might say that almost everyone can, if attentive, learn to navigate in Jersey City, but only at the cost of some effort and uncertainty. Moreover, the positive values of legible surroundings are missing: the emotional satisfaction, the framework for communication or conceptual organization, the new depths that it may bring to everyday experience. These are pleasures we lack, even if our present city environment is not so disordered as to impose an intolerable strain on those who are familiar with it.

Jersey City is discussed in Chapter 2

It must be granted that there is some value in mystification, labyrinth, or surprise in the environment. Many of us enjoy the House of Mirrors, and there is a certain charm in the crooked streets of Boston. This is so, however, only under two conditions. First, there must be no danger of losing basic form or orientation, of never coming out. The surprise must occur in an over-all framework; the confusions must be small regions in a visible whole. Furthermore, the labyrinth or mystery must in itself have some form that can be explored and in time be apprehended. Complete chaos without hint of connection is never pleasurable.

These points are further illustrated in Appendix A

But these second thoughts point to an important qualification. The observer himself should play an active role in perceiving the world and have a creative part in developing his image. He should have the power to change that image to fit changing needs. An environment which is ordered in precise and final detail may inhibit new patterns of activity. A landscape whose every rock tells a story may make difficult the creation of fresh stories. Although this may not seem to be a critical issue in our present urban chaos, yet it indicates that what we seek is not a final but an open-ended order, capable of continuous further development.

Building the Image

Environmental images are the result of a two-way process between the observer and his environment. The environment suggests distinctions and relations, and the observer—with great adaptability and in the light of his own purposes—selects, organizes, and endows with meaning what he sees. The image so developed now limits and emphasizes what is seen, while the image itself is being tested against the filtered perceptual input in a constant interacting process. Thus the image of a given reality may vary significantly between different observers.

The coherence of the image may arise in several ways. There may be little in the real object that is ordered or remarkable, and yet its mental picture has gained identity and organization through long familiarity. One man may find objects easily on what seems to anyone else to be a totally disordered work table. Alternatively, an object seen for the first time may be identified and related not because it is individually familiar but because it conforms to a stereotype already constructed by the observer. An American can always spot the corner drugstore, however indistinguishable it might be to a Bushman. Again, a new object may seem to have strong structure or identity because of striking physical features which suggest or impose their own pattern. Thus the sea or a great mountain can rivet the attention of one coming from the flat plains of the interior, even if he is so young or so parochial as to have no name for these great phenomena.

As manipulators of the physical environment, city planners are primarily interested in the external agent in the interaction which produces the environmental image. Different environments resist or facilitate the process of image-making. Any given form, a fine vase or a lump of clay, will have a high or a low probability of evoking a strong image among various observers. Presumably this probability can be stated with greater and greater precision as the observers are grouped in more and more homogeneous classes of age, sex, culture, occupation, temperament, or familiarity. Each individual creates and bears his own image, but there seems to be substantial agreement among members of the same group. It is these group images, exhibiting consensus among significant numbers, that interest city planners who aspire to model an environment that will be used by many people.

Therefore this study will tend to pass over individual differences, interesting as they might be to a psychologist. The first order of business will be what might be called the "public images," the common mental pictures carried by large numbers of a city's inhabitants: areas of agreement which might be expected to appear in the interaction of a single physical reality, a common culture, and a basic physiological nature.

The systems of orientation which have been used vary widely throughout the world, changing from culture to culture, and from landscape to landscape. Appendix A gives examples of many of them: the abstract and fixed directional systems, the moving systems, and those that are directed to the person, the home, or the sea. The world may be organized around a set of focal points, or be broken into named regions, or be linked by remembered routes. Varied as these methods are, and inexhaustible as seem to be the potential clues which a man may pick out to differentiate his world, they cast interesting side-lights on the means that we use today to locate ourselves in our own city world. For the most part these examples seem to echo, curiously enough, the formal types of image elements into which we can conveniently divide the city image: path, landmark, edge, node, and district. These elements will be defined and discussed in Chapter 3.

Structure and Identity

An environmental image may be analyzed into three components: identity, structure, and meaning. It is useful to abstract these for analysis, if it is remembered that in reality they always appear together. A workable image requires first the identification of an object, which implies its distinction from other things, its recognition as a separable entity. This is called identity, not in the sense of equality with something else, but with the meaning of individuality or oneness. Second, the image must include the spatial or pattern relation of the object to the observer and to other objects. Finally, this object must have some meaning for the observer, whether practical or emotional. Meaning is also a relation, but quite a different one from spatial or pattern relation.

Thus an image useful for making an exit requires the recognition of a door as a distinct entity, of its spatial relation to the observer, and its meaning as a hole for getting out. These are not truly separable. The visual recognition of a door is matted together with its meaning as a door. It is possible, however, to analyze the door in terms of its identity of form and clarity of position, considered as if they were prior to its meaning.

Such an analytic feat might be pointless in the study of a door, but not in the study of the urban environment. To begin with, the question of meaning in the city is a complicated one. Group images of meaning are less likely to be consistent at this level than are the perceptions of entity and relationship. Meaning, moreover, is not so easily influenced by physical manipulation as are these other two components. If it is our purpose to build cities for the enjoyment of vast numbers of people of widely diverse background—and cities which will also be adaptable to future purposes—we may even be wise to concentrate on the physical clarity of the image and to allow meaning to develop without our direct guidance. The image of the Manhattan skyline may stand for vitality, power, decadence, mystery, congestion, greatness, or what you will, but in each case that sharp picture crystallizes and reinforces the meaning. So various are the individual meanings of a city, even while its form may be easily communicable, that it appears possible to separate meaning from form, at least in the early stages of analysis. This study will therefore concentrate on the identity and structure of city images.

If an image is to have value for orientation in the living space, it must have several qualities. It must be sufficient, true in a pragmatic sense, allowing the individual to operate within his environment to the extent desired. The map, whether exact or not, must be good enough to get one home. It must be sufficiently clear and well integrated to be economical of mental effort: the map must be readable. It should be safe, with a surplus of clues so that alternative actions are possible and the risk of failure is not too high. If a blinking light is the only sign for a critical turn, a power failure may cause disaster. The image should preferably be open-ended, adaptable to change, allowing the individual to continue to investigate and organize reality: there should be blank spaces where he can extend the drawing for himself. Finally, it should in some measure be communicable to other individuals. The relative importance of these criteria for a "good" image will vary with different persons in different situations; one will prize an economical and sufficient system, another an open-ended and communicable one.

Imageability

Since the emphasis here will be on the physical environment as the independent variable, this study will look for physical qualities which relate to the attributes of identity and structure in the mental image. This leads to the definition of what might be called *imageability:* that quality in a physical object which gives it a high probability of evoking a strong image in any given observer. It is that shape, color, or arrangement which facilitates the making of vividly identified, powerfully structured, highly useful mental images of the environment. It might also be called *legibility,* or perhaps *visibility* in a heightened sense, where objects are not only able to be seen, but are presented sharply and intensely to the senses.

Half a century ago, Stern discussed this attribute of an artistic object and called it *apparency*.[74] While art is not limited to this single end, he felt that one of its two basic functions was "to create images which by clarity and harmony of form fulfill the need for vividly comprehensible appearance." In his mind, this was an essential first step toward the expression of inner meaning.

A highly imageable (apparent, legible, or visible) city in this peculiar sense would seem well formed, distinct, remarkable; it would invite the eye and the ear to greater attention and participation. The sensuous grasp upon such surroundings would not merely be simplified, but also extended and deepened. Such a city would be one that could be apprehended over time as a pattern of high continuity with many distinctive parts clearly interconnected. The perceptive and familiar observer could absorb new sensuous impacts without disruption of his basic image, and each new impact would touch upon many previous elements. He would be well oriented, and he could move easily. He would be highly aware of his environment. The city of Venice might be an example of such a highly imageable environment. In the United States, one is tempted to cite parts of Manhattan, San Francisco, Boston, or perhaps the lake front of Chicago.

These are characterizations that flow from our definitions. The concept of imageability does not necessarily connote something fixed, limited, precise, unified, or regularly ordered, although it may sometimes have these qualities. Nor does it mean apparent at a glance, obvious, patent, or plain. The total environment to be patterned is highly complex, while the obvious image is soon boring, and can point to only a few features of the living world.

The imageability of city form will be the center of the study to follow. There are other basic properties in a beautiful environment: meaning or expressiveness, sensuous delight, rhythm, stimulus, choice. Our concentration on imageability does not deny their importance. Our purpose is simply to consider the need for identity and structure in our perceptual world, and to illustrate the special relevance of this quality to the particular case of the complex, shifting urban environment.

Since image development is a two-way process between observer and observed, it is possible to strengthen the image either by symbolic devices, by the retraining of the perceiver, or by reshaping one's surroundings. You can provide the viewer with a symbolic diagram of how the world fits together: a map or a set of written instructions. As long as he can fit reality to the diagram, he has a clue to the relatedness of things. You can even install a machine for giving directions, as has recently been done in New York.[49] While such devices are extremely useful for providing condensed data on interconnections, they are also precarious, since orientation fails if the device is lost, and the device itself must constantly be referred and fitted to reality. The cases of brain injury noted in Appendix A illustrate the anxiety and effort that attend complete reliance on such means. Moreover, the complete experience of interconnection, the full depth of a vivid image, is lacking.

You may also train the observer. Brown remarks that a maze through which subjects were asked to move blindfolded seemed to them at first to be one unbroken problem. On repetition, parts of the pattern, particularly the beginning and end, became familiar and assumed the character of localities. Finally, when they could tread the maze without error, the whole system seemed to have become one locality.[8] DeSilva describes the case of a boy who seemed to have "automatic" directional orientation, but proved to have been trained from infancy (by a mother who could not distinguish right from left) to respond to "the east side of the porch" or "the south end of the dresser."[71]

Shipton's account of the reconnaissance for the ascent of Everest offers a dramatic case of such learning. Approaching Everest from a new direction, Shipton immediately recognized the main peaks and saddles that he knew from the north side. But the Sherpa guide accompanying him, to whom both sides were long familiar, had never realized that these were the same features, and he greeted the revelation with surprise and delight.[70]

Kilpatrick describes the process of perceptual learning forced on an observer by new stimuli that no longer fit into previous images.[41] It begins with hypothetical forms that explain the new stimuli conceptually, while the illusion of the old forms persists.

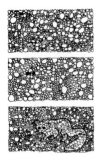

The personal experience of most of us will testify to this persistence of an illusory image long after its inadequacy is conceptually realized. We stare into the jungle and see only the sunlight on the green leaves, but a warning noise tells us that an animal is hidden there. The observer then learns to interpret the scene by singling out "give-away" clues and by reweighting previous signals. The camouflaged animal may now be picked up by the reflection of his eyes. Finally by repeated experience the entire pattern of perception is changed, and the observer need no longer consciously search for give-aways, or add new data to an old framework. He has achieved an image which will operate successfully in the new situation, seeming natural and right. Quite suddenly the hidden animal appears among the leaves, "as plain as day."

In the same way, we must learn to see the hidden forms in the vast sprawl of our cities. We are not accustomed to organizing and imaging an artificial environment on such a large scale; yet our activities are pushing us toward that end. Curt Sachs gives an example of a failure to make connections beyond a certain level.[64] The voice and drumbeat of the North American Indian follow entirely different tempos, the two being perceived independently. Searching for a musical analogy of our own, he mentions our church services, where we do not think of coordinating the choir inside with the bells above.

In our vast metropolitan areas we do not connect the choir and the bells; like the Sherpa, we see only the sides of Everest and not the mountain. To extend and deepen our perception of the environment would be to continue a long biological and cultural development which has gone from the contact senses to the distant senses and from the distant senses to symbolic communications. Our thesis is that we are now able to develop our image of the environment by operation on the external physical shape as well as by an internal learning process. Indeed, the complexity of our environment now compels us to do so. Chapter 4 will discuss how this might be done.

Primitive man was forced to improve his environmental image by adapting his perception to the given landscape. He could effect minor changes in his environment with cairns, beacons, or tree blazes, but substantial modifications for visual clarity or visual interconnection were confined to house sites or religious enclosures. Only powerful civilizations can begin to act on their total environment at a significant scale. The conscious remolding of the large-scale physical environment has been possible only recently, and so the problem of environmental imageability is a new one. Technically, we can now make completely new landscapes in a brief time, as in the Dutch polders. Here the designers are already at grips with the question of how to form the total scene so that it is easy for the human observer to identify its parts and to structure the whole.[30]

We are rapidly building a new functional unit, the metropolitan region, but we have yet to grasp that this unit, too, should have its corresponding image. Suzanne Langer sets the problem in her capsule definition of architecture:

"It is the total environment made visible."[42]

II.

THREE CITIES

To understand the role of environmental images in our own urban lives, it was necessary for us to look carefully at some city areas and to talk with their inhabitants. We needed to develop and test the idea of imageability, and also by a comparison of image with visual reality to learn what forms make for strong images, and thus to suggest some principles for urban design. The work was done in the conviction that analysis of existing form and its effects on the citizen is one of the foundation stones of city design, and in the hope that some useful techniques for field reconnaissance and citizen interview might be developed as a by-product. As in any small pilot study, the purpose was to develop ideas and methods, rather than to prove facts in a final and determinate way.

Analyses were therefore made of the central areas of three American cities: Boston, Massachusetts; Jersey City, New Jersey; and Los Angeles, California. Boston, the city directly at hand, is unique in character among American cities, being both vivid in form and full of locational difficulties. Jersey City was chosen for its apparent formlessness, for what seemed, on first observation, to be its extremely low order of imageability. Los Angeles, on the other hand, is a new city, of an utterly different scale, and with a gridiron plan in its central area. In every case a central area of approximately 2½ by 1½ miles was taken for study. In each of these cities, two basic analyses were carried out:

1. A systematic field reconnaissance of the area was made on foot by a trained observer, who mapped the presence of various elements, their visibility, their image strength or weakness, and their connections, disconnections, and other interrelations, and who noted any special successes or difficulties in the potential image structure. These were subjective judgments based on the immediate appearance of these elements in the field.

For details, see Appendix B

2. A lengthy interview was held with a small sample of city residents to evoke their own images of their physical environment. The interview included requests for descriptions, locations, and sketches, and for the performance of imaginary trips. The persons interviewed were people who were long resident or employed in the area, and whose residences or work places were distributed throughout the zone in question.

Some thirty persons were thus interviewed in Boston, and fifteen each in Jersey City and Los Angeles. In Boston the basic analyses were supplemented by photographic recognition tests, by actual trips in the field, and by numerous requests for directions made of passers-by in the streets. In addition, detailed field reconnaissance was made of several special elements of the Boston scene.

All these methods are described and evaluated in Appendix B. The small size of the samples and their bias toward the professional and managerial classes prevent us from stating that a true "public image" has been gained. But the material is rich in suggestion, and has sufficient internal consistency to indicate that substantial group images do exist and are, in part at least, discoverable by some such means. The independent field analyses predicted rather accurately the group image derived from the interviews, and so indicated the role of the physical forms themselves.

Undoubtedly, the common concentrations of travel paths or of work place tended to produce this consistency of the group image by presenting the same elements to the view of many individuals. Associations of status or of history, coming from non-visual sources, further reinforced these likenesses.

, But there can be no doubt that the form of the environment itself played a tremendous role in the shaping of the image. The coincidences of description, of vividness, even of confusion where familiarity would seem to indicate knowledge, all make this clear. It is on this relation between image and physical form that our interest centers.

Distinct differences in the imageability of the three cities appeared, even though the persons interviewed had all made some sort of a working adjustment to their environment. Certain features—open space, vegetation, sense of motion on the paths, visual contrasts—seemed to be of particular importance in the cityscape.

From the data provided by the comparison of these group images with the visual reality, and from the speculations arising thereon, most of the remainder of this book derives. The concepts of imageability and of the element types (which will be discussed in Chapter 3) largely derive from, or were refined and developed in, the analysis of this material. While a discussion of the strengths and weaknesses of the methods are left to Appendix B, it is important to understand the basis on which the work rests.

Boston

The area chosen for study in Boston was all that part of the central peninsula within the line of Massachusetts Avenue. This is an area rather unusual among American cities because of its age, history, and somewhat European flavor. It includes the commercial core of the metropolitan area, as well as several high-density residential districts, ranging from slum to upper-class housing. Figure 1 is a general aerial view of the region, Figure 2 is an outline map of it, and Figure 3 is a diagrammatic representation of its major visual elements as derived from the field reconnaissance.

Figure 1

Figure 2, page 18

Figure 3, page 19

For almost all the persons interviewed, this Boston is a city of very distinctive districts and of crooked, confusing paths. It is a dirty city, of red-brick buildings, symbolized by the open space of the Boston Common, the State House with its gold dome, and the view across the Charles River from the Cambridge side. Most of them added that it is an old, historical place, full of worn-out buildings, yet containing some new structures among the old. Its narrow streets are congested with people and cars; there is no parking space, but there are striking contrasts between wide main streets and narrow side streets. The central city is a peninsula, surrounded by a water edge. In addition to the Common, the Charles River, and the State House, there are several other vivid elements, particularly Beacon Hill, Commonwealth Avenue, the Washington Street shopping and theater district,

FIG. 1. *The Boston peninsula from the north*

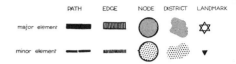
Copley Square, the Back Bay, Louisburg Square, the North End, the market district, and Atlantic Avenue bordered by the wharves. A substantial fraction added other characteristics about Boston: that it lacks open or recreational space; that it is an "individual," small, or medium-sized city; that it has large areas of mixed use; or that it is marked by bay windows, iron fences, or brownstone fronts.

The favorite views were usually the distant panoramas with the sense of water and space. The view from across the Charles River was often cited, and there were mentions of the river view down Pinckney Street, the vista from a hill in Brighton, the look of Boston from its harbor. Another favorite sight was that of

Figure 4, page 20

FIG. 2. *Outline map of the Boston peninsula*

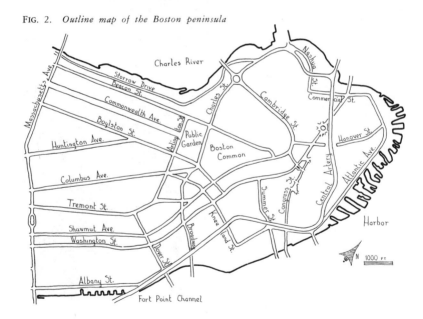

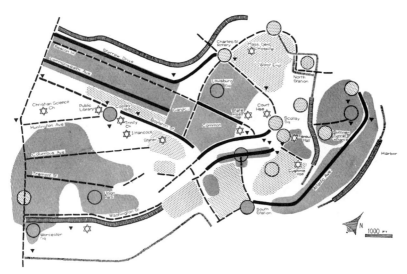

FIG. 3. *The visual form of Boston as seen in the field*

the city lights at night, from near or far, when the city seems to take on an excitement that it normally lacks.

Boston has a structure which is understood by almost all of these people. The Charles River with its bridges makes a strong clear edge to which the principal Back Bay streets, particularly Beacon Street and Commonwealth Avenue, are parallel. These streets spring from Massachusetts Avenue, itself perpendicular to the Charles, and run to the Boston Common and Public Garden. Alongside this set of Back Bay streets is Copley Square, into which runs Huntington Avenue.

Figure 5, page 21

On the lower side of the Common are Tremont and Washington Streets, parallel to each other and interconnected by several smaller streets. Tremont Street goes as far as Scollay Square, and from this joint or node Cambridge Street runs back to another node at the Charles Street rotary which ties the framework back in to the river again. In so doing, it encloses Beacon Hill. Farther away from the river appears another strong water edge, Atlantic Avenue and the harbor front, which may be only

FIG. 4. *Boston from across the Charles River*

uncertainly connected to the rest. Although many subjects had an intellectual conception of Boston as a peninsula, they were unable to make a visual connection between river and harbor. Boston seems in some ways to be a "one-sided" city, which loses precision and content as one moves away from the Charles River edge.

If our sample is representative, almost any Bostonian can tell you this much of his city. Equally likely, he could *not* describe some other things, such as the triangular area between the Back Bay and the South End, the no-man's land south of North Station, how Boylston Street runs into Tremont Street, or what is the pattern of paths in the financial district.

Figure 35, page 146

One of the most interesting districts is one that isn't there: the triangular region between the Back Bay and the South End. This was a blank area on the map for every person interviewed, even the one who was born and raised there. It is an area of substantial size containing some known elements such as Huntington Avenue and occasional landmarks such as the Christian Science Church, but the matrix in which these might appear is absent and nameless. Presumably, the blocking by surrounding railroad tracks, and the conceptual squeezing-out of this area because the main streets of Back Bay and the South End are felt to be parallel, both contribute to this disappearance.

The Boston Common, on the other hand, is for many subjects the core of their image of the city, and, along with Beacon Hill, the Charles River, and Commonwealth Avenue, is most often mentioned as a particularly vivid place. Often, in making their cross-city trips, people would veer off course to touch base here as they went by. A large, planted open space bordering the most intensive district in Boston, a place full of associations, accessible to all, the Common is quite unmistakable. It is so located as to expose one edge of three important districts: Beacon Hill, the Back Bay, and the downtown shopping district, and is therefore a nucleus from which anyone can expand his knowledge of the environment. Furthermore, it is highly differentiated within itself, including the little subway plaza, the fountain, the Frog Pond, the bandstand, the cemetery, the "swan pond," and so on.

At the same time this open space has a most peculiar shape, difficult to remember: a five-sided, right-angled figure. Since it is also too large and well planted for the sides to be intervisible, people are often at sea in trying to cross it. And since two of the bounding paths, Boylston and Tremont Streets, are of city-

Figure 6, page 23

FIG. 5. *The Boston that everyone knows*

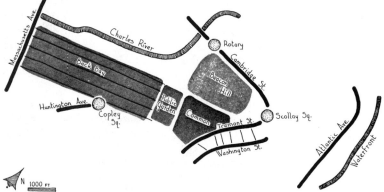

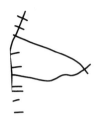

wide importance, the difficulty is compounded. Here they cross at right angles, but farther out they seem to be parallel, springing perpendicularly from a common base line, Massachusetts Avenue. In addition, the central shopping activity makes an awkward right-angled turn at this same Boylston-Tremont crossing, weakens, and then reappears farther up Boylston Street. All this adds up to a critical ambiguity of shape at the city core, a major orientation flaw.

Boston is a city of distinctive districts, and in most parts of the central area one knows where one is simply by the general character of the surrounding area. In one portion there is the unusual case of a continuous mosaic of such distinctive areas: the sequence Back Bay—Common—Beacon Hill—central shopping. Here place is never in question. Yet this thematic vividness is typically associated with formlessness or confusing arrangement. If Boston districts could be given structural clarity as well as distinctive character, they would be greatly strengthened. In this failure, incidentally, Boston is probably quite different from many American cities, where areas of formal order have little character.

While the districts tend to be vivid, the path system in Boston is generally confused. Nevertheless, so important is the function of circulation that the paths are still dominant in the total image, just as in the other cities tested. There is no basic order among these paths, except for the historically conditioned preponderance of main radials running inwards from the base of the peninsula. Through much of the central city it is easier to move east-west to and from Massachusetts Avenue than it is to move at right angles to this direction. In this sense, the city has a sort of grain that is reflected in the mental contortions which accompany various imaginary trips. Nevertheless, the path structure is an unusually difficult one, and its complications have furnished much material for the systematic consideration of paths in Chapter 3. The difficulty caused by the right-angled crossing of "parallel" Boylston and Tremont Streets has already been mentioned. The regular Back Bay grid, a banal characteristic of most American cities, takes on a special quality in Boston by virtue of its contrast with the remainder of the pattern.

FIG. 6. *The Boston Common*

Two high-speed highways pass through the central area, Storrow Drive and the Central Artery. Both are felt ambiguously either as barriers in reference to movement on the older streets, or as paths when one imagines oneself to be driving on them. Each aspect has an entirely different face: when thought of from below, the Artery is a massive green-painted wall, appearing fragmentarily at certain spots. As a path, it is a ribbon rising, dipping, and turning, studded with signs. In a curious way, both roads are felt to be "outside" the city, hardly related to it, even though they penetrate it, and there is a dizzying transition to be made at each interchange. Storrow Drive, however, is clearly related to the Charles River, and is thus tied to the general pattern of the city. The Central Artery, on the other hand, winds inexplicably through the center, and breaks the orientation link with the North End by blocking Hanover Street. Moreover, it was sometimes confused with the Causeway-Commercial-Atlantic sequence, even though the two paths are quite different, because both may logically be considered as extensions of Storrow Drive.

Figure 7, page 24

FIG. 7. *The Central Artery*

FIG. 8. *Problems of the Boston image*

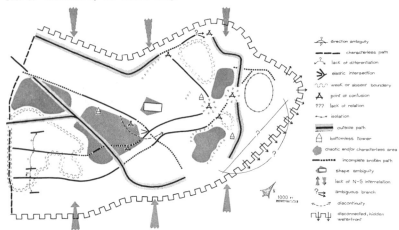

In good Boston fashion, individual parts of the path system may have strong character. But this highly irregular system is made up of separate elements which are only linked one by one, or sometimes not at all. It is a difficult system to draw, or to image as a whole, and must usually be handled by concentrating on the sequence of joints. These joints or nodes are therefore quite important in Boston, and often rather pallid regions like the "Park Square area" will be named by the crossing that is their organizing focus.

Figure 8 is one way of summarizing this analysis of the Boston image, a summary which might be a first step toward the preparation of a design plan. It is a graphic compilation of what seem to be the major difficulties in the city image: confusions, floating points, weak boundaries, isolations, breaks in continuity, ambiguities, branchings, lacks of character or differentiation. Coupled with a presentation of the strengths and potentialities of the image, it corresponds to the site-analysis phase of a plan on a smaller scale. Like a site analysis, it does not determine a plan but is the background upon which creative decisions can be made. Since it is made at a more comprehensive level of analysis, it quite naturally contains a larger degree of interpretation than do previous diagrams.

Figure 8

Jersey City

Jersey City, New Jersey, lies between Newark and New York City, and is a fringe area of both, with little central activity of its own. Crisscrossed by railroads and elevated highways, it has the appearance of a place to pass through rather than to live in. It is divided into ethnic and class neighborhoods, and is cut by the ramparts of the Palisades. What might have been its natural shopping center was stifled by the artificial creation of Journal Square on the upper land, so that the city has no single center, but rather four or five. To the usual formlessness of space and heterogeneity of structure that mark the blighted area of any American city is added the complete confusion of an uncoordinated street system. The drabness, dirt, and smell of the town are at first overpowering. This, of course, is the first super-

Figure 9, page 27

ficial view of an outsider. It was interesting to see how those who had lived there for many years imaged it for themselves.

The visual structure of Jersey City as derived from the field reconnaissance is drawn to the same scale and uses the same symbols as the Boston diagram. The city has a little more shape and pattern than an outsider might think, as indeed it must if it is to be habitable at all. But it has rather little and boasts of many fewer recognized elements than does the same area of Boston. Much of the area is disrupted by strong edges. The essentials of the structure are Journal Square, one of the two main shopping centers, with the line of Hudson Boulevard passing through it. From Hudson Boulevard depends the "Bergen Section" and the important West Side Park. To the east, three paths pass down over the cliff edge to more or less converge in the lower area: Newark, Montgomery, and Communipaw-Grand. On the cliff stands the Medical Center. Everything stops at the barrier of the railroad-industrial-dock area on the Hudson. This is the essential pattern, and, except perhaps for one or two of the three downhill streets, is familiar to most subjects.

The lack of character is apparent from a glance when the consensus of elements thought distinctive by Jersey City people is compared with the same diagram for Boston. The Jersey City map is almost bare. Journal Square is strong because of its intensive shopping and entertainment activity, but its traffic and spatial chaos are confusing and unsettling. Hudson Boulevard rivals the Square for strength; West Side Park is next, the only large park in the city, cited again and again as a distinctive region, a relief in the general texture. The "Bergen Section" stands out primarily as a class area. The New Jersey Medical Center is visually unmistakable, rising tall and white from the edge of the cliff, a haphazardly located giant.

Little more can be cited as distinctive with any unanimity, except for the awe-inspiring sight of the New York City skyline

Figure 10

Figures 37 and 41, pages 147 and 149

Figure 11, page 28

Figure 12, page 28

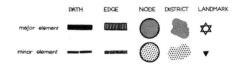

	PATH	EDGE	NODE	DISTRICT	LANDMARK
major element					
minor element					

FIG. 9. *Jersey City from the south*

FIG. 10. *The visual form of Jersey City as seen in the field*

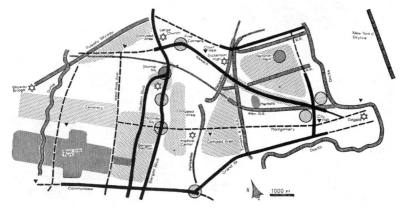

27

FIG. 11. *Journal Square*

FIG. 12. *The New Jersey Medical Center*

in the distance. The other diagrams fill out the image of the city, adding in particular those practical necessities, the major paths, primarily the well-trafficked ones which by their continuity are the exceptions to the majority of Jersey City streets. There is a paucity of recognizable districts and landmarks, and a lack of commonly known centers or nodal points. The city is, however, marked by the presence of several strong edges or isolating boundaries: the overhead lines of railroads and highways, the Palisades, and the two waterfronts.

In studying the individual sketches and interviews, it became apparent that none of the respondents had anything like a comprehensive view of the city in which they had lived for many years. The maps were often fragmented, with large blank areas, concentrating most often on small home territories. The river bluff seemed to be a strong isolating element, and usually a map showed either the top as strong and the lowland as weak or, vice versa, the two being connected by one or two purely conceptual paths. The lower area, in particular, seemed difficult to structure.

When asked for a general characterization of the city, one of the most common remarks was that it was not a whole, that it had no center, but was rather a collection of many hamlets. The question: "What first comes to mind with the words 'Jersey City'?," so easy to answer for Bostonians, proved to be a difficult one. Again and again, subjects repeated that "nothing special" came to mind, that the city was hard to symbolize, that it had no distinctive sections. One woman put it:

This is really one of the most pitiful things about Jersey City. There isn't anything that if someone came here from a far place, that I could say, "Oh, I want you to see this, this is so beautiful."

The most common response to the question of symbolism was nothing in the city at all, but rather the sight of the New York City skyline across the river. Much of the characteristic feeling for Jersey City seemed to be that it was a place on the edge of something else. One person put it that his two symbols were the skyline of New York, on the one side, and the Pulaski Skyway, standing for Newark, on the other. Another emphasized the sense of enclosing barriers: that to get out of Jersey City one must either go under the Hudson, or through the confusing Tonnelle traffic circle.

One could hardly ask for a more dramatic, more imageable, basic location and piece of topography than Jersey City, if one were able to build completely anew. But the general environment was persistently referred to with the words "old," "dirty," "drab." The streets were repeatedly described as "cut up." The interviews were notable for their paucity of information about the environment, and for the conceptual, rather than perceptually concrete, quality of the city image. Most striking was the strong tendency to describe, not by visual images, but by street names and the types of use. Take the following part of a trip description in a familiar area, as an example:

> After you cross the highway, there's a going-up bridge; and after you come under the bridge, the first street you get to, there's a tannery packing company; the second corner after going on the avenue, you see banks on each side; and you come to the next corner, there's a radio store and a hardware store right close together on your right. On your left, before you cross the street, is a grocery store and a cleaner. You come on up to 7th Street, and on 7th Street is a saloon facing you on the lefthand corner, a vegetable market on the righthand — a liquor store on the right side of the road, on the left is a grocery store. The next street is 6th Street; there's no landmark except that you come under the railroad again. When you go under the railroad, the next street is 5th. On your right is a saloon; there's a new filling station across the street on your right; there is a saloon on the left. 4th Street — when you come to 4th on the righthand corner, there's a vacant lot; next to that vacant lot is a saloon; on the righthand side facing you is a meat wholesale place; and on your left across from the meat place, is a glass store. The next is 3rd — you come up to 3rd and see a drugstore on your right, whiskey store across from you on the right; on the left is a grocery store and a saloon on your left across from the grocery store. The next is 2nd, and there's a grocery store on the left and a saloon on the left across from it. On your right, before you cross the street, there's a place where they sell household appliances, and then 1st Street, there's a butcher shop, meat market on the left and across from it is a vacant lot that's used for a parking lot, on your right is a clothing store and a candy store on the right. . . .

and so on. In all this description we have only one or two visual images: a "going-up" bridge, and perhaps the railroad underpass. This subject first seems to see her environment when she reaches Hamilton Park, and then through her eyes one suddenly catches a glimpse of the fenced, open square, with its round, central bandstand, and the surrounding benches.

Many remarks came out about the indistinguishability of the physical scene:

> It's much the same all over . . . it's more or less just commonness to me. I mean, when I go up and down the streets, it's more or less the same thing — Newark Avenue, Jackson Avenue, Bergen Avenue. I mean, sometimes you can't decide which avenue you want to go on, because they're more or less just the same; there's nothing to differentiate them.
>
> How would I recognize Fairview Avenue when I come to it?

FIG. 13. *A street in Jersey City*

By the street sign. It's the only way you can recognize any street in this city. There's nothing distinctive, just another apartment house, that's all, on the corner.

I think we usually find our way around. Where there's a will there's a way. It's confusing at times, you may lose some minutes in trying to find a place, but I think eventually you get where you want to go to.

In this relatively undifferentiated environment there is a reliance not only on use-locations, but frequently on gradients of use, or of the relative state of repair of structures. The street signs, the big advertising signs of Journal Square, and the factories are the landmarks. Any landscaped open spaces, such as Hamilton or Van Vorst Parks, or especially the large West Side Park, are cherished. On two occasions, people used tiny grass triangles at certain street intersections as landmarks. Another woman spoke of driving over to a small park on a Sunday, so that she could sit in the car and look at it. The fact that the Medical Center has a small landscaped plot in front of it seems to be as important an identifying characteristic as its great bulk and skyline silhouette.

The evident low imageability of this environment was reflected in the image held even by its long-time residents, and was manifested in dissatisfaction, poor orientation, and an inability to describe or differentiate its parts. Yet even such a seemingly chaotic set of surroundings does in fact have some pattern, and people seize upon and elaborate this pattern by concentration on minor clues, as well as by shifting their attention from physical appearance to other aspects.

Los Angeles

The Los Angeles area, the heart of a great metropolitan region, presents a different picture, and one quite different from Boston as well. The area, while comparable in size to the Boston and Jersey City zones, includes little more than the central business district and its fringes. The subjects were familiar with the area, not through residence, but by reasons of work place in one of the central offices or stores. Figure 14 presents the field reconnaissance in the usual manner.

Figure 14

As the core of a metropolis, central Los Angeles is heavily charged with meaning and activity, with large and presumably distinctive buildings, and with a basic pattern: its almost regular grid of streets. Yet a number of factors operate to result in a different, and less sharp, image than that of Boston. First is the decentralization of the metropolitan region, whereby the central area is still by courtesy "downtown," but there are several other basic cores to which people are oriented. The central area has intensive shopping, but it is no longer the best shopping, and great numbers of citizens never enter the downtown area from one year to the next. Second, the grid pattern itself is an undifferentiated matrix, within which elements cannot always be located with confidence. Third, the central activities are spatially extended and shifting, a fact which dilutes their impact. Fre-

FIG. 14. *The visual form of Los Angeles as seen in the field*

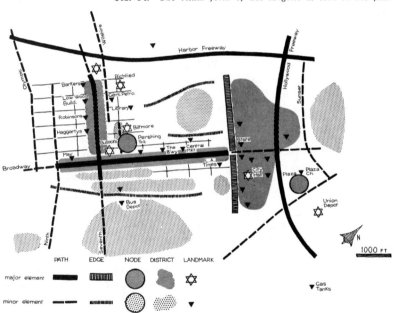

FIG. 15. *Los Angeles from the west*

Figure 15

quent rebuilding prevents the identification that builds up by historical process. The elements themselves, despite (and sometimes because of) frequent attempts at flamboyance, are often visually faceless. Nevertheless, we are not now looking at another chaotic Jersey City, but rather at the active and ecologically ordered center of a great metropolis.

The accompanying aerial photograph gives an impression of this scene. Except by minute attention to plant types, or to the distant background, it would be hard to distinguish this from the center of many U. S. cities. There is the same piling-up of blank office structures, the same ubiquity of traffic ways and parking lots. The image maps, however, are much more dense than those of Jersey City.

The essential structure of this image is the nodal point of Pershing Square, which lies in the crook of the L formed by two shopping streets, Broadway and 7th Street. All this is in the general matrix of a grid of paths. At the far end of Broadway is the Civic Center area, and beyond that the sentimentally important node of the Plaza-Olvera Street. Alongside Broadway is the

Spring Street financial district, and next over is Skid Row (Main Street). The Hollywood and Harbor Freeways may be recognized as bounding the two open sides of the L. The general image is remarkable for its emptiness east of Main or Los Angeles Streets, and south of 7th Street, except for the extension of the repeating grid. The central area is set in a vacuum. This L-shaped center is liberally sprinkled with remembered landmarks, chief of them being the Statler and Biltmore Hotels, and then, among others, the Richfield Building, the Public Library, Robinsons and Bullocks department stores, the Federal Savings Building, the Philharmonic auditorium, City Hall, and the Union Depot. But only two landmarks were described in any concrete detail: the ugly, black and gold Richfield Building and the pyramided top of the City Hall.

Figure 43, page 150

FIG. 16. *The Civic Center*

FIG. 17. *Pershing Square*

Other than the Civic Center area, recognizable districts are either small and linear, confined to the borders of paths (such as the 7th Street shopping, the Broadway shopping, Transportation Row on 6th Street, the Spring Street financial district, and Skid Row on Main Street), or relatively weak: Bunker Hill, Little Tokyo. The Civic Center is strongest, because of its obvious function, size, spatial openness, new buildings, and definite edges. Few fail to remark it. Bunker Hill is not as strong an image, despite its historical connotations, and quite a few felt that it was "not in the downtown area." Indeed, it is surprising how the core, in bending around this major topographic feature, has succeeded in visually burying it.

Figure 16, page 35

Pershing Square is consistently the strongest element of all: an exotically landscaped open space in the heart of downtown, reinforced by its use as an outdoor political forum, camp meeting,

and old people's rest. Along with the Plaza-Olvera Street node *Figure 17*
(involving another open space), Pershing Square was the most
sharply described element, with its immaculate central lawn,
fringed first by banana trees, then by a ring of old people sitting
in solid ranks on the stone walls, then by busy streets, and finally
by the close files of downtown buildings. Although remarkable,
it was not always felt to be pleasant. Sometimes subjects showed
fear of the old and eccentric people who use it; more often the
response was one of pathos, heightened by the way in which these
people are confined to the fringing walls, and kept off the central grass. Unfavorable comparisons were drawn with the earlier,
if dowdier, aspect of the Square: a grove of trees, with scattered
benches and walks. The central grass was resented not only because of its denial to the park loungers, but because it makes it
impossible to cut across the space, as a pedestrian would normally
do. Nevertheless, this is a highly identifiable image, strengthened by the presence of a dominant landmark, the red-brown
mass of the Biltmore Hotel, which efficiently orients the direction
of the Square.

For all its importance in the city image, Pershing Square seems
to float a little. It is one block away from the two key streets,
7th and Broadway, and many were uncertain of its precise location, although sure of its general one. Subjects on their trips
tended in their minds to peer sideways for it, as they passed each
minor street. This seems bound up with its off-center location,
and also with the subjects' tendency to confound various streets,
as noted below.

Broadway was perhaps the only path which was unmistakable
for all. As the original main street and still the largest shopping *Figure 18, page 38*
concentration in the downtown area, it is marked by the crowds
on its sidewalks, by the length and continuity of its shopping, by
the marquees of its movie houses, and by the street cars (where
other streets carry only busses). Although conceded to be the
core, if anything is, yet Broadway was not a shopping area for
most of these middle-class persons. Its walks are crowded with
the ethnic minorities and lower-income groups whose living
quarters ring the central section. The subjects interviewed
regarded this linear core as an alien one, looking at it with vary-

ing degrees of avoidance, curiosity, or fear. They were quick to describe the status differences between the Broadway crowds, and those to be seen on 7th Street, which, if not elite, is at least a middle-class shopping street.

In general, it is difficult to differentiate the numbered cross streets one from another, except for 6th, 7th, and 1st Streets. This confusion of paths was apparent in the interviews. To a lesser extent, the named longitudinal streets were also interchangeable. Several of these "north-south" streets, particularly Flower, Hope, Grand, and Olive, all of which run into Bunker Hill, tended at times, like the numbered streets, to be confused one for another.

Although one downtown street may be confounded for another, few subjects had difficulty in maintaining direction on the paths. End vistas, such as the Statler Hotel on 7th Street, the Library on Hope Street, Bunker Hill on Grand Street; and

FIG. 18. *Broadway*

side-to-side differences in use or pedestrian intensity, such as along Broadway, seem frequent enough to provide directional differentiation. In fact all streets are visually closed, despite the regular grid at the center, whether by topography, the freeways, or an irregularity in the grid itself.

Across the Hollywood Freeway is one of the strongest elements of all, the nodal center of the Plaza-Olvera Street. This was very sharply described: its shape, trees, benches, people; the tiles, the "cobbled" (actually brick-paved) street, the tight space, the goods for sale, unfailingly the smells of candles and candy. Not only is this small spot visually very distinct, but it is the only true historical anchor-point in the city and seems to generate a fierce attachment.

Through this same general area, however, between the Union Depot and the Civic Center, subjects had great difficulty in picking their way. They felt that the grid had deserted them, and

Figure 19

FIG. 19. *The Plaza and the entrance to Olvera Street*

Figure 20

they were unsure where the known streets struck into this amorphous zone. Alameda Street leads treacherously away to the left, instead of paralleling the north-south streets. The large-scale clearance of the civic area seems to have erased the original grid and substituted little new. The freeway is a sunken barrier. In their task of walking from Union Depot to the Statler, the relief with which most subjects greeted the appearance of 1st Street was almost audible.

When asked to describe or symbolize the city as a whole, the subjects used certain standard words: "spread-out," "spacious," "formless," "without centers." Los Angeles seemed to be hard to envision or conceptualize as a whole. An endless spread, which may carry pleasant connotations of space around the dwellings, or overtones of weariness and disorientation, was the common image. Said one subject:

FIG. 20. *The Hollywood Freeway*

It's as if you were going somewhere for a long time, and when you got there you discovered there was nothing there, after all.

But there was some evidence that orientation at the regional scale was not too difficult. The apparatus of regional orientation included the ocean, the mountains and hills for the older residents, the valley regions such as San Fernando and the large development districts such as Beverly Hills, the major freeway and boulevard system, and, finally, a central gradient of age over the whole metropolis, evidenced in the condition, style, and type of structures appropriate to each era in the successive rings of growth. Below this grand scale, however, structure and identity seemed to be quite difficult. There were no medium-sized districts, and paths were confused. People spoke of being lost when off habitual routes, of depending heavily on street signs. At the smallest scale, there were occasional pockets of high identity and meaning: mountain cabins, beach houses, or areas planted with highly differentiated vegetation. But this was not universal, and an essential middle link in the structure, the imageability of districts at the medium scale, tended to be weak.

In almost all the interviews, where subjects were describing the trip they took from home to work, there was a progressive decrease in the vividness of impressions as they approached downtown. Near the home there was much detail about the slopes and turns, the vegetation and the people; there was evidence of daily interest and pleasure in the scene. Nearing the center, this image gradually became grayer, more abstract and conceptual. The downtown area, as in Jersey City, was basically a collection of named uses and store fronts. Undoubtedly this was in part due to the increasing strain of driving on the major radials, but it seemed to persist even after leaving the car. Evidently the visual material is itself of poorer stuff. Perhaps the increasing smog also has its effect.

Smog and haze, incidentally, were frequently mentioned as the torment of the city dweller. They seemed to dull environmental colors, so that the over-all tone was reported to be whitish, yellowish, or gray. Several drivers into the city center reported that they regularly checked on smog conditions each morning, by noting the visibility of such distant tower beacons as the Richfield Building, or City Hall.

Automobile traffic and the highway system were dominant themes in the interviews. This was the daily experience, the daily battle—sometimes exciting, usually tense and exhausting. Trip details were full of references to signal lights and signs, intersections and turning problems. On the freeways, decisions had to be made far ahead of time; there were constant lane maneuvers. It was like shooting rapids in a boat, with the same excitement and tension, the same constant effort to "keep one's head." Many subjects noted their fears on driving a new route for the first time. There were frequent references to the overpasses, the fun of the big interchanges, the kinesthetic sensations of dropping, turning, climbing. For some persons, driving was a challenging, high-speed game.

Figure 20, page 40

On these fast roads, one can have some sense of the major topography. One subject felt that coming over a great hill each morning marked the midpoint of her journey and gave shape to it. Another noted the extension of the city's scale due to the new roads, which have changed her whole conception of the relations of elements. There were references to the pleasure of momentary extensive views from elevated portions of the freeway, versus the contained monotonous sensation of the embankment in a cut. On the other hand, as in Boston, these drivers seemed to have difficulty in locating the freeway, in tying it to the rest of the city structure. There was a common experience of a momentary loss of orientation when coming off a freeway ramp.

Another frequent theme was that of relative age. Perhaps because so much of the environment is new or changing, there was evidence of widespread, almost pathological, attachment to anything that had survived the upheaval. Thus the tiny Plaza-Olvera Street node, or even the decayed hotels of Bunker Hill, claimed the attention of many subjects. There was an impression from these few interviews that there is an even greater sentimental attachment to what is old than exists in conservative Boston.

In Los Angeles as well as in Jersey City, people took great delight in flowers and vegetation, which indeed are the glory of many of the residential sections of the city. The early portions of home-to-work trips were full of vivid pictures of the flowers and trees. Even car drivers moving at high speed seemed to note and enjoy such urban detail. But these remarks did not apply to the area directly under study. Central Los Angeles is far from the visual chaos of Jersey City, and it has a rather liberal number of single building landmarks. Yet, except for a conceptual and rather undifferentiated grid, it was difficult to organize or comprehend as a whole. It had no strong general symbols. The strongest images, Broadway and Pershing Square, were, to this middle class group of subjects at least, rather alien or even menacing. Not one described them as pleasant or beautiful. The little, neglected Plaza, and certain of the shopping or entertainment functions symbolized by the landmarks in the upper 7th Street area were the only elements on which any affection was bestowed. One subject put this by saying that the old Plaza, on one end, and the new Wilshire Boulevard, on the other, were the only things with character, and that they summed up Los Angeles. The image seemed to lack much of the recognizable character, stability, and pleasant meaning of central Boston.

Common Themes

We find, in comparing these three cities (if we can find anything in such small samplings) that, as might be expected, people adjust to their surroundings and extract structure and identity out of the material at hand. The types of elements used in the city image, and the qualities that make them strong or weak, seem quite comparable between the three, although the proportion of element types may vary with the actual form. Yet at the same time, there are marked differences between the levels of orientation and satisfaction in these different physical environments.

Among other things, the tests made clear the significance of space and breadth of view. The dominance of Boston's Charles River edge is based on the wide visual sweep it affords on entering the city from this side. A large number of city elements can be seen at once in their relations; one's position relative to the whole is abundantly clear. Los Angeles' Civic Center was noted for its spatial openness; Jersey City subjects responded to

Figure 4, page 20

the view before them as they descended the Palisades toward the Manhattan skyline.

There was an emotional delight arising from a broad view, which was referred to many times. Would it be possible, in our cities, to make this panoramic experience a more common one, for the thousands who pass every day? A broad view will sometimes expose chaos, or express characterless loneliness, but a well-managed panorama seems to be a staple of urban enjoyment. Even raw or shapeless space seems to be remarkable, although perhaps not pleasant. Many people refer to the clearance and excavation at Dewey Square in Boston as a striking sight. Undoubtedly this is by contrast to the otherwise tight urban spaces. But when the space has some form, as it does along the Charles River or on Commonwealth Avenue, in Pershing Square or Louisburg Square or to some extent in Copley Square, the impact is much stronger: the feature becomes memorable. If Boston's Scollay Square or Jersey City's Journal Square had spatial character commensurate with their functional importance, they would truly be key features in their cities.

The landscape features of the city: the vegetation or the water, were often noted with care and with pleasure. The Jersey City subjects were sharply aware of the few green oases in their surroundings; those of Los Angeles often stopped to describe the exotic variety of local vegetation. Several of them reported daily detours which lengthened their trip to work but allowed them to pass by some particular planting, park, or body of water. Here is a not unusual excerpt from a Los Angeles trip:

> You cross over Sunset, past a little park — I don't know what the name of it is. It's very nice, and — oh — the jacarandas are coming into bloom. One house about a block above has them. On down Canyon and all kinds of palm trees there: the high palms and the low palms; and then on down to the park.

Los Angeles, geared to the motor car, also furnishes the most vivid examples of the response to the path system: to the way it is itself organized, to its relation with other city elements, to its own internal character of space, view, and motion. But the visual dominance of the paths and their key influence as the network from which most people experience their surroundings are also amply attested to in the Boston and Jersey City material.

Quite as apparent is the constant reference to socio-economic class: the avoidance of "lower class" Broadway in Los Angeles, the recognition of the "upper class" Bergen Section in Jersey City, or the unmistakable division of Boston's Beacon Hill into two distinct sides.

The interviews brought out another general response: to the way in which the physical scene symbolizes the passage of time. The Boston interviews were full of references to age contrast: the "new" Artery cutting through the "old" market district; the new Catholic chapel among the ancient buildings on Arch Street; the old (dark, ornamented, low) Trinity Church silhouetted against the new (bright, stark, tall) John Hancock Building, and so on. Indeed, descriptions were often made as if they were a response to contrast in the urban scene: spatial contrast, status contrast, use contrast, relative age, or comparisons of cleanliness or of landscaping. Elements and attributes became remarkable in terms of their setting in the whole.

In Los Angeles there is an impression that the fluidity of the environment and the absence of physical elements which anchor to the past are exciting and disturbing. Many descriptions of the scene by established residents, young or old, were accompanied by the ghosts of what used to be there. Changes, such as those wrought by the freeway system, have left scars on the mental image. The interviewer remarked:

There seems to be a bitterness or nostalgia among natives which could be resentment at the many changes, or just inability to reorient fast enough to keep up with them.

General comments such as these quickly become apparent on reading the interview material. It is possible, however, to study both interviews and field studies more systematically, and to learn much more about the character and structure of the urban image. This will be the burden of the following chapter.

45

III.

THE CITY IMAGE AND ITS ELEMENTS

There seems to be a public image of any given city which is the overlap of many individual images. Or perhaps there is a series of public images, each held by some significant number of citizens. Such group images are necessary if an individual is to operate successfully within his environment and to cooperate with his fellows. Each individual picture is unique, with some content that is rarely or never communicated, yet it approximates the public image, which, in different environments, is more or less compelling, more or less embracing.

This analysis limits itself to the effects of physical, perceptible objects. There are other influences on imageability, such as the social meaning of an area, its function, its history, or even its name. These will be glossed over, since the objective here is to uncover the role of form itself. It is taken for granted that in actual design form should be used to reinforce meaning, and not to negate it.

The contents of the city images so far studied, which are referable to physical forms, can conveniently be classified into five types of elements: paths, edges, districts, nodes, and landmarks.

Indeed, these elements may be of more general application, since they seem to reappear in many types of environmental images, as may be seen by reference to Appendix A. These elements may be defined as follows:

1. *Paths.* Paths are the channels along which the observer customarily, occasionally, or potentially moves. They may be streets, walkways, transit lines, canals, railroads. For many people, these are the predominant elements in their image.  People observe the city while moving through it, and along these paths the other environmental elements are arranged and related.

2. *Edges.* Edges are the linear elements not used or considered as paths by the observer. They are the boundaries between two phases, linear breaks in continuity: shores, railroad cuts, edges of development, walls. They are lateral references rather than coordinate axes. Such edges may be barriers, more or less penetrable, which close one region off from another; or they may be seams, lines along which two regions are related and joined together. These edge elements, although probably not as dominant as paths, are for many people important organizing features, particularly in the role of holding together generalized areas, as in the outline of a city by water or wall.

3. *Districts.* Districts are the medium-to-large sections of the city, conceived of as having two-dimensional extent, which the observer mentally enters "inside of," and which are recognizable as having some common, identifying character. Always identifiable from the inside, they are also used for exterior reference if  visible from the outside. Most people structure their city to some extent in this way, with individual differences as to whether paths or districts are the dominant elements. It seems to depend not only upon the individual but also upon the given city.

4. *Nodes.* Nodes are points, the strategic spots in a city into which an observer can enter, and which are the intensive foci to and from which he is traveling. They may be primarily junctions, places of a break in transportation, a crossing or convergence of paths, moments of shift from one structure to another. Or the nodes may be simply concentrations, which gain their importance from being the condensation of some use or physical character, as a street-corner hangout or an enclosed square. Some

of these concentration nodes are the focus and epitome of a district, over which their influence radiates and of which they stand as a symbol. They may be called cores. Many nodes, of course, partake of the nature of both junctions and concentrations. The concept of node is related to the concept of path, since junctions are typically the convergence of paths, events on the journey. It is similarly related to the concept of district, since cores are typically the intensive foci of districts, their polarizing center. In any event, some nodal points are to be found in almost every image, and in certain cases they may be the dominant feature.

5. *Landmarks*. Landmarks are another type of point-reference, but in this case the observer does not enter within them, they are external. They are usually a rather simply defined physical object: building, sign, store, or mountain. Their use involves the singling out of one element from a host of possibilities. Some landmarks are distant ones, typically seen from many angles and distances, over the tops of smaller elements, and used as radial references. They may be within the city or at such a distance that for all practical purposes they symbolize a constant direction. Such are isolated towers, golden domes, great hills. Even a mobile point, like the sun, whose motion is sufficiently slow and regular, may be employed. Other landmarks are primarily local, being visible only in restricted localities and from certain approaches. These are the innumerable signs, store fronts, trees, doorknobs, and other urban detail, which fill in the image of most observers. They are frequently used clues of identity and even of structure, and seem to be increasingly relied upon as a journey becomes more and more familiar.

The image of a given physical reality may occasionally shift its type with different circumstances of viewing. Thus an expressway may be a path for the driver, and edge for the pedestrian. Or a central area may be a district when a city is organized on a medium scale, and a node when the entire metropolitan area is considered. But the categories seem to have stability for a given observer when he is operating at a given level.

None of the element types isolated above exist in isolation in the real case. Districts are structured with nodes, defined by edges, penetrated by paths, and sprinkled with landmarks. Elements regularly overlap and pierce one another. If this analysis begins with the differentiation of the data into categories, it must end with their reintegration into the whole image. Our studies have furnished much information about the visual character of the element types. This will be discussed below. Only to a lesser extent, unfortunately, did the work make revelations about the interrelations between elements, or about image levels, image qualities, or the development of the image. These latter topics will be treated at the end of this chapter.

Paths

For most people interviewed, paths were the predominant city elements, although their importance varied according to the degree of familiarity with the city. People with least knowledge of Boston tended to think of the city in terms of topography, large regions, generalized characteristics, and broad directional relationships. Subjects who knew the city better had usually mastered part of the path structure; these people thought more in terms of specific paths and their interrelationships. A tendency also appeared for the people who knew the city best of all to rely more upon small landmarks and less upon either regions or paths.

The potential drama and identification in the highway system should not be underestimated. One Jersey City subject, who can find little worth describing in her surroundings, suddenly lit up when she described the Holland Tunnel. Another recounted her pleasure:

> You cross Baldwin Avenue, you see all of New York in front of you, you see the terrific drop of land (the Palisades) . . . and here's this open panorama of lower Jersey City in front of you and you're going down hill, and there you know: there's the tunnel, there's the Hudson River and everything. . . . I always look to the right to see if I can see the . . . Statue of Liberty. . . . Then I always look up to see the Empire State Building, see how the weather is. . . . I have a real feeling of happiness because I'm going someplace, and I love to go places.

Particular paths may become important features in a number of ways. Customary travel will of course be one of the strongest influences, so that major access lines, such as Boylston Street, Storrow Drive, or Tremont Street in Boston, Hudson Boulevard in Jersey City, or the freeways in Los Angeles, are all key image features. Obstacles to traffic, which often complicate the structure, may in other cases clarify it by concentrating cross flow into fewer channels, which thus become conceptually dominant. Beacon Hill, acting as a giant rotary, raises the importance of Cambridge and Charles Streets; the Public Garden strengthens Beacon Street. The Charles River, by confining traffic to a few highly visible bridges, all of individual shape, undoubtedly clarifies the path structure. Quite similarly, the Palisades in Jersey City focus attention on the three streets that successfully surmount it.

Figure 30, page 77

Concentration of special use or activity along a street may give it prominence in the minds of observers. Washington Street is the outstanding Boston example: subjects consistently associated it with shopping and theatres. Some people extended these characteristics to parts of Washington Street that are quite different (e.g., near State Street); many people seemed not to know that Washington extends beyond the entertainment segment, and thought it ended near Essex or Stuart Streets. Los Angeles has many examples—Broadway, Spring Street, Skid Row, 7th Street —where the use concentrations are prominent enough to make linear districts. People seemed to be sensitive to variations in the amount of activity they encountered, and sometimes guided themselves largely by following the main stream of traffic. Los

Figure 18, page 38

Angeles' Broadway was recognized by its crowds and its street cars; Washington Street in Boston was marked by a torrent of pedestrians. Other kinds of activity at ground level also seemed to make places memorable, such as construction work near South Station, or the bustle of the food markets.

Characteristic spatial qualities were able to strengthen the image of particular paths. In the simplest sense, streets that suggest extremes of either width or narrowness attracted attention. Cambridge Street, Commonwealth Avenue, and Atlantic Avenue are all well known in Boston, and all were singled out for their great width. Spatial qualities of width and narrowness derived part of their importance from the common association of main streets with width and side streets with narrowness. Looking for, and trusting to the "main" (i.e., wide) street becomes automatic, and in Boston the real pattern usually supports this assumption. Narrow Washington Street is the exception to this rule, and here the contrast is so strong in the other direction, as narrowness is reinforced by tall buildings and large crowds, that the very reversal became the identifying mark. Some of the orientation difficulties in Boston's financial district, or the anonymity of the Los Angeles grid, may be due to this lack of spatial dominance. Special façade characteristics were also important for path identity. Beacon Street and Commonwealth Avenue were distinctive partly because of the building façades that line them. Pavement texture seemed to be less important, except in special cases such as Olvera Street in Los Angeles. Details of planting seemed also to be relatively unimportant, but a great deal of planting, like that on Commonwealth Avenue, could reinforce a path image very effectively.

Figure 21, page 53

Proximity to special features of the city could also endow a path with increased importance. In this case the path would be acting secondarily as an edge. Atlantic Avenue derived much importance from its relation to the wharves and the harbor, Storrow Drive from its location along the Charles River. Arlington and Tremont Streets were distinctive because one side runs along a park, and Cambridge Street acquired clarity from its border relationship to Beacon Hill. Other qualities that gave importance to single paths were the visual exposure of the path itself or the visual exposure from the path of other parts of the city. The Central Artery was notable partly for its visual prominence as it sweeps through the city on an elevated course. The bridges over the Charles were also apparent for long distances. But the Los Angeles freeways at the edges of the downtown area are visually concealed by cuts or planted embankments. A number of car-oriented subjects spoke as if those freeways were not there. On the other hand, drivers indicated that their attention sharpened as a freeway came out of a cut and attained a wide view.

Figure 7, page 24

Figure 20, page 40

Occasionally, paths were important largely for structural reasons. Massachusetts Avenue was almost pure structure for most subjects, who were unable to describe it. Yet its relationship as an intersector of many confusing streets made it a major Boston element. Most of the Jersey City paths seemed to have this purely structural character.

Where major paths lacked identity, or were easily confused one for the other, the entire city image was in difficulty. Thus Tremont Street and Shawmut Avenue might be interchangeable in Boston, or Olive, Hope, and Hill Streets in Los Angeles. Boston's Longfellow Bridge was not infrequently confused with the Charles River Dam, probably since both carry transit lines and terminate in traffic circles. This made for real difficulties in the city, both in the road and subway systems. Many of the paths in Jersey City were difficult to find, both in reality and in memory.

That the paths, once identifiable, have continuity as well, is an obvious functional necessity. People regularly depended upon this quality. The fundamental requirement is that the actual track, or bed of the pavement, go through; the continuity of other characteristics is less important. Paths which simply have a satisfactory degree of track continuity were selected as the dependable ones in an environment like Jersey City. They can be followed by the stranger, even if with difficulty. People often generalized that other kinds of characteristics along a continuous track were also continuous, despite actual changes.

But other factors of continuity had importance as well. When the channel width changed, as Cambridge Street does at Bowdoin Square, or when the spatial continuity was interrupted, as it is at Washington Street at Dock Square, people had difficulty in sensing a continuation of the same path. At the other end of Washington Street, a sudden change in the use of buildings may partly explain why people failed to extend Washington Street beyond Kneeland Street into the South End.

Examples of characteristics giving continuity to a path are the planting and façades along Commonwealth Avenue, or the building type and setback along Hudson Boulevard. Names in themselves played a role. Beacon Street is primarily in the Back Bay but relates to Beacon Hill by its name. The continuity of the name of Washington Street gave people a clue as to how to proceed through the South End, even if they were ignorant of this area. There is a pleasant feeling of relationship to be gained

FIG. 21. *Commonwealth Avenue*

simply from standing on a street which by name continues to the heart of the city, however far. A reverse example is the attention given to the nondescript beginnings of Wilshire and Sunset Boulevards in the central area of Los Angeles, because of their special character farther out. The path bordering the Boston harbor, on the other hand, was at times fragmented simply because of the changing names it bears: Causeway Street, Commercial Street, and Atlantic Avenue.

Paths may not only be identifiable and continuous, but have directional quality as well: one direction along the line can easily be distinguished from the reverse. This can be done by a gradient, a regular change in some quality which is cumulative in one direction. Most frequently sensed were the topographic gradients: in Boston, particularly on Cambridge Street, Beacon Street, and Beacon Hill. A gradient of use intensity, such as on the approach to Washington Street, was also noted, or, on a regional scale, the gradient of increasing age on approaching the center of Los Angeles on a freeway. In the relatively gray environment of Jersey City, there were two examples of gradients based on the relative state of repair of tenements.

A prolonged curve is also a gradient, a steady change in direction of movement. This was not often sensed kinesthetically: the only citations of a bodily sense of curving motion were in the Boston subway, or on portions of the Los Angeles freeways. When street curves are mentioned in the interviews, they seem to relate primarily to visual clues. The turning in Charles Street at Beacon Hill was sensed, for example, because the close building walls heightened the visual perception of curvature.

People tended to think of path destinations and origin points: they liked to know where paths came from and where they led. Paths with clear and well-known origins and destinations had stronger identities, helped tie the city together, and gave the observer a sense of his bearings whenever he crossed them. Some subjects thought of general destinations for paths, to a section of the city, for example, while others thought of specific places. One person, who made rather high demands for intelligibility upon the city environment, was troubled because he saw a set of railroad tracks, and did not know the destination of trains using them.

Cambridge Street in Boston has clear, strategic terminal points: the Charles Street rotary and Scollay Square. Other streets may have only one sharp terminal: Commonwealth Avenue at the Public Garden, or Federal Street at Post Office Square. On the other hand, the indefinite finale of Washington Street—variously thought of as going to State Street, to Dock Square, to Haymarket Square, or even to North Station (actually it formally runs to the Charlestown bridge)—prevented it from becoming as strong a feature as it might otherwise have been. In Jersey City, the never-accomplished convergence of the three main streets crossing the Palisades, and their final nondescript subsidence, was highly confusing.

This same kind of end-from-end differentiation, which is conferred by termini, can be created by other elements which may be visible near the end, or apparent end, of a path. The Common near one end of Charles Street acted this way, as did the State House for Beacon Street. The apparent visual closure of 7th Street in Los Angeles by the Hotel Statler, and of Boston's Washington Street by the Old South Meeting House, had the same effect. Both are accomplished by a slight shift of the path direction, putting an important building on the visual axis. Elements known to be on a particular side of a path also conferred a sense of direction: Symphony Hall on Massachusetts Avenue and the Boston Common along Tremont Street were both employed in this way. In Los Angeles, even the relatively heavier concentration of pedestrians on the western side of Broadway was used to judge in which direction one was facing.

Figure 32, page 80

Figure 18, page 38

Once a path has directional quality, it may have the further attribute of being scaled: one may be able to sense one's position along the total length, to grasp the distance traversed or yet to go. Features which facilitate scaling, of course, usually confer a sense of direction as well, except for the simple technique of counting blocks, which is directionless but can be used to compute distances. Many subjects referred to this latter clue, but by no means all. It was most commonly used in the regular pattern of Los Angeles.

Most often, perhaps, scaling was accomplished by a sequence of known landmarks or nodes along the path. The marking of identifiable regions as a path enters and leaves them also constituted a powerful means of giving direction and scaling to a path. Charles Street entering Beacon Hill from the Common, and Summer Street entering the shoe and leather district on the way to South Station, are examples of this effect.

Given a directional quality in a path, we may next inquire if it is aligned, that is, if its direction is referable to some larger

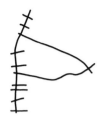

system. In Boston, there were many examples of unaligned paths. One common cause was the subtle, misleading curve. Most people missed the curve in Massachusetts Avenue at Falmouth Street, and confused their total map of Boston as a result. They considered Massachusetts Avenue to be straight, sensed its right-angle intersections with a large number of streets, and assumed these streets to be parallel. Boylston and Tremont Streets were difficult because, by a number of small changes, they pass over from almost parallel to almost perpendicular. Atlantic Avenue was elusive because it is a compound of two long curves and a substantial straight tangent, a path which completely reverses its direction but is straight in its most characteristic section.

At the same time more abrupt directional shifts may enhance visual clarity by limiting the spatial corridor, and by providing prominent sites for distinctive structures. Thus the Washington Street core was defined; Hanover Street was crowned by an old church at the apparent end; and the South End cross streets gained intimacy as they shifted course to cross the major radials. Quite similarly, one was prevented from sensing the vacuum in which central Los Angeles is placed by the grid shifts which close off the outward view.

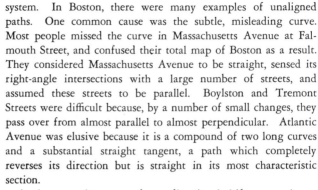

The second common cause of misalignment to the rest of the city was the sharp separation of a path from surrounding elements. Paths in the Boston Common, for example, caused much confusion: people were uncertain which walkways to use in order to arrive at particular destinations outside the Common. Their view of these outside destinations was blocked, and the paths of the Common failed to tie to outside paths. The Central

Figure 7, page 24

Artery was a still better example, for it is more detached from its surroundings. It is elevated and does not allow a clear view of adjacent streets, but permits a kind of fast and undisturbed movement totally missing in the city. It is a special kind of automobile-land rather than a normal city street. Many subjects had great difficulty aligning the Artery to surrounding elements, although it was known to connect North and South Stations. In Los Angeles as well, the freeways were not felt to be "in" the rest of the city, and coming off an exit ramp was typically a moment of severe disorientation.

Recent research on the problems of erecting directional signs on the new freeways has shown that this disassociation from the surroundings causes each turning decision to be made under pressure and without adequate preparation. Even familiar drivers showed a surprising lack of knowledge of the freeway system and its connections. General orientation to the total landscape was the greatest need of these motorists.[2]

The railroad lines and the subway are other examples of detachment. The buried paths of the Boston subway could not be related to the rest of the environment except where they come up for air, as in crossing the river. The surface entrances of the stations may be strategic nodes in the city, but they are related along invisible conceptual linkages. The subway is a disconnected nether world, and it is intriguing to speculate what means might be used to mesh it into the structure of the whole.

Figure 29, page 75

The water surrounding the Boston peninsula is a basic element to which parts may be aligned. The Back Bay grid was related to the Charles River; Atlantic Avenue was linked to the harbor; Cambridge Street led clearly to the river from Scollay Square. Hudson Boulevard in Jersey City, despite its frequent twists, was aligned with the long peninsula between the Hackensack and the Hudson. The Los Angeles grid, of course, provided automatic alignment between downtown streets. It was easy to put down as a basic pattern in a sketch map, even if the individual streets were not distinguishable. Two-thirds of the subjects drew this first, before adding any other elements. However, the fact that this grid is turned through some angular distance, both from the ocean coast line and the cardinal directions, gave a number of subjects some uneasiness.

When we consider more than one path, then the path intersection becomes vital, since it is the point of decision. The simple perpendicular relationship seemed easiest to handle, especially if the shape of the intersection was reinforced by other features. The best-known intersection in Boston, according to our interviews, was that of Commonwealth Avenue and Arlington Street. It is a visually obvious tee, supported by the space, the planting, the traffic, and the importance of the elements joined. The crossing of Charles and Beacon Streets was also well known: the outlines are made visible and reinforced by the borders of the Common and the Public Garden. Intersections of a number of streets with Massachusetts Avenue were easily understood, probably because the right-angle relationships stood out in contrast to the remainder of the central city.

Indeed, for several subjects, confused intersections with streets entering from many angles were one of their typical Boston characteristics. Crossings of more than four points almost always gave trouble. An experienced taxi dispatcher, with a near-perfect grasp of the city path structure, confessed that the five-pointed crossing at Church Green on Summer Street was one of the two things in the city that troubled him. Equally unnerving was a traffic circle with many entering paths occurring at rapid intervals around an undifferentiated curve.

But the number of entrances is not the whole story. Even a non-perpendicular, five-pointed crossing may be made clear, as has been done in Boston's Copley Square. The controlled space ·and the heightened character of the node serve to bring out the angled relationship between Huntington Avenue and Boylston Street. Park Square, on the other hand, is a simple perpendicular joint that in its shapelessness fails to communicate its structure. At many Boston crossings not only are the number of paths multiplied, but the continuity of the spatial corridor is completely lost when it strikes the chaotic emptiness of a square.

Nor are such chaotic crossings simply the product of past historical accident. The contemporary highway interchange is even more confusing, particularly since it must be negotiated at higher speeds. Several Jersey City subjects, for example, spoke with fear of the shape of the Tonnelle Avenue Circle.

Figure 22

A perceptual problem on a larger scale is raised where a path branches slightly to make alternate paths, both of relative importance. A case is the branching of Storrow Drive (after a name confusion with Charles Street) into two paths: the older Nashua Street, leading to Causeway-Commercial-Atlantic, and the recent Central Artery. These two paths were not infrequently confused with one another, producing major convulsions in the image. All subjects seemed unable to conceive both at once: maps showed either one or the other as an extension of Storrow Drive. Quite similarly, in the subway system, the successive

branching of main lines was a problem, since it was hard to keep
distinct the images of two slightly divergent branches and hard
to remember where the branch occurred.

A few important paths may be imaged together as a simple
structure, despite any minor irregularities, as long as they have
a consistent general relationship to one another. The Boston
street system is not conducive to this kind of image, except perhaps for the basic parallelism of Washington and Tremont
Streets. But the Boston subway system, whatever its involutions
in true scale, seemed fairly easy to visualize as two parallel lines
cut at the center by the Cambridge-Dorchester line, although the
parallel lines might be confused one with the other, particularly
since both go to North Station. The freeway system in Los

FIG. 22. *The Tonnelle Avenue Circle*

Angeles seemed to be imaged as a complete structure, as did the Jersey City system of Hudson Boulevard intersected by three paths which go down over the Palisades, or the triad of West Side, Hudson, and Bergen Boulevards, with the regular cross streets between.

Where a subject was accustomed to travel by automobile, one-way restrictions were difficult complications in the image of a path structure. The taxi dispatcher's second mental block was due to just such an irreversibility in the system. For others, Washington Street was not traceable across Dock Square because it is one-way entering on both sides.

A large number of paths may be seen as a total network, when repeating relationships are sufficiently regular and predictable.

FIG. 23. *The Back Bay*

The Los Angeles grid is a good example. Almost every subject could easily put down some twenty major paths in correct relation to each other. At the same time, this very regularity made it difficult for them to distinguish one path from another. Boston's Back Bay is an interesting path network. Its regularity is remarkable in contrast to the rest of the central city, an effect that would not occur in most American cities. But this is not a featureless regularity. The longitudinal streets were sharply differentiated from the cross streets in everyone's mind, much as they are in Manhattan. The long streets all have individual character—Beacon Street, Marlboro Street, Commonwealth Avenue, Newbury Street, each one is different—while the cross streets act as measuring devices. The relative width of the streets, the block lengths, the building frontages, the naming system, the relative length and number of the two kinds of streets, their functional importance, all tend to reinforce this differentiation. Thus a regular pattern is given form and character. The alphabet formula for naming the cross streets was frequently used as a location device, much as the numbers are used in Los Angeles.

Figure 23

The South End, on the other hand, while having the same topological form of long parallel major streets interconnected by short minor streets, and while often mentally considered as a regular grid, is much less successful in its pattern. Major and minor streets are also differentiated by width and use, and many of the minor streets have more character than those of the Back Bay. But there is a lack of differentiated character in the major streets: Columbus Avenue is hard to distinguish from Tremont Street, or from Shawmut Avenue. This interchangeability was frequent in the interviews.

The frequent reduction of the South End to a geometrical system was typical of the constant tendency of the subjects to impose regularity on their surroundings. Unless obvious evidence refuted it, they tried to organize paths into geometrical networks, disregarding curves and non-perpendicular intersections. The lower area of Jersey City was frequently drawn as a grid, even though it is one only in part. Subjects absorbed all of central Los Angeles into a repeating network, without being disturbed by the distortion at the eastern edge. Several subjects even insisted on reducing the street maze of Boston's financial district to a checkerboard! The sudden, and particularly the rather indiscernible, shift of one grid system to another grid system, or to a non-grid, was very confusing. Subjects in Los Angeles were often quite disoriented in the area north of First Street or east of San Pedro.

Edges

Edges are the linear elements not considered as paths: they are usually, but not quite always, the boundaries between two kinds of areas. They act as lateral references. They are strong in Boston and Jersey City but weaker in Los Angeles. Those edges seem strongest which are not only visually prominent, but also continuous in form and impenetrable to cross movement. The Charles River in Boston is the best example and has all of these qualities.

The importance of the peninsular definition of Boston has already been mentioned. It must have been much more important in the 18th century, when the city was a true and very striking peninsula. Since then the shore lines have been erased or changed, but the picture persists. One change, at least, has *Figure 4, page 20* strengthened the image: the Charles River edge, once a swampy backwater, is now well defined and developed. It was frequently described, and sometimes drawn in great detail. Everyone remembered the wide open space, the curving line, the bordering highways, the boats, the Esplanade, the Shell.

The water edge on the other side, the harborfront, was also generally known, and remembered for its special activity. But the sense of water was less clear, since it was obscured by many structures, and since the life has gone out of the old harbor activities. Most subjects were unable to interconnect the Charles River and Boston Harbor in any concrete way. Partly this must be due to the screening of the water at the tip of the peninsula by railroad yards and buildings, partly to the chaotic aspect of the water, with its myriad bridges and docks, at the meeting of the Charles River, the Mystic River, and the sea. The lack of frequented waterside paths, as well as the drop in water level at the Dam, also breaks the continuity. Farther west, few were aware of any

water in the South Bay, nor could they imagine any stop to development in this direction. This lack of peninsular closure deprived the citizen of a satisfying sense of completion and rationality in his city.

The Central Artery is inaccessible to pedestrians, at some points impassable, and is spatially prominent. But it is only occasionally exposed to view. It was a case of what might be called a fragmentary edge: in the abstract continuous, but only visualized at discrete points. The railroad lines were another example. The Artery, in particular, was like a snake lying over the city image. Held down at the ends and at one or two internal points, it elsewhere writhed and twisted from one position to the next. The lack of relation felt while driving the Artery was mirrored in its ambiguous location for the pedestrian.

Figure 7, page 24

Storrow Drive, on the other hand, while also felt to be "outside" by the driver, was clearly located on the map, because of its alignment to the Charles River. It was the Charles River, despite its role as the basic edge in the Boston image, which was curiously isolated from the detailed structure of the adjoining Back Bay. People were at a loss as to how to move from one to the other. We can speculate that this was not true before Storrow Drive cut off pedestrian access at the foot of each cross street.

Similarly, the interrelation of the Charles River and Beacon Hill was hard to grasp. Although the position of the hill is potentially explanatory of the puzzling bend in the river, and although the hill thereby gains a commanding enfilade view of the river edge, the Charles Street rotary seemed for most people to be the only firm connection between the two. If the hill rose sharply and immediately out of the water, instead of behind a masking foreshore covered by uses which are only doubtfully associated with Beacon Hill, and if it were more closely tied to the path system along the river, then the relation would have been much clearer.

In Jersey City, the waterfront was also a strong edge, but a rather forbidding one. It was a no-man's land, a region beyond the barbed wire. Edges, whether of railroads, topography, throughways, or district boundaries, are a very typical feature of this environment and tend to fragment it. Some of the most

FIG. 24. *The lake front of Chicago*

unpleasant edges, such as the bank of the Hackensack River with
its burning dump areas, seemed to be mentally erased.

The disruptive power of an edge must be reckoned with. The
isolation of the North End in Boston by the Central Artery was
glaring, in the eyes of residents and non-residents alike. Had it
been possible, for example, to preserve the connection of Hanover
Street into Scollay Square, this effect might have been minimized,
The widening of Cambridge Street, in its day, must have done
the same to the West End-Beacon Hill continuum. The broad
gash of Boston's railroad tracks seemed to dismember the city,
and to isolate the "forgotten triangle" between the Back Bay and
the South End.

While continuity and visibility are crucial, strong edges are not necessarily impenetrable. Many edges are uniting seams, rather than isolating barriers, and it is interesting to see the differences in effect. Boston's Central Artery seems to divide absolutely, to isolate. Wide Cambridge Street divides two regions sharply but keeps them in some visual relation. Beacon Street, the visible boundary of Beacon Hill along the Common, acts not as a barrier but as a seam along which the two major areas are clearly joined together. Charles Street at the foot of Beacon Hill *Figure 57, page 169* both divides and unites, leaving the lower area in uncertain relation to the hill above. Charles Street carries heavy traffic but also contains the local service stores and special activities associated with the Hill. It pulls the residents together by attracting them to itself. It acts ambiguously either as linear node, edge, or path for various people at various times.

Edges are often paths as well. Where this was so, and where the ordinary observer was not shut off from moving on the path (as he is on the Central Artery, for example), then the circulation image seemed to be the dominant one. The element was usually pictured as a path, reinforced by boundary characteristics.

Figueroa and Sunset Streets, and to a lesser extent Los Angeles and Olympic Streets, were usually thought of as the edges of the Los Angeles central business district. Interestingly enough, they were stronger in this respect than the Hollywood and Harbor Freeways, which also can be thought of as major boundaries, and are both much more important as paths and physically more imposing. The fact that Figueroa and the other surface streets are conceptually part of the general grid, and have been familiar for some time, as well as the relative invisibility of the depressed or landscaped freeways, all conspired to erase these freeways from the image. Many subjects had difficulty in making a mental connection between the fast highway and the remainder ot the city structure, just as in the Boston case. They would, in imagination, even walk across the Hollywood Freeway as if it did not exist. A high-speed artery may not necessarily be the best way of visually delimiting a central district.

The elevated railways of Jersey City and Boston are examples of what might be called overhead edges. The elevated along

Washington Street in Boston, seen from below, identifies the path and fixes the direction to downtown. Where it leaves the street, at Broadway, the path loses direction and force. When several such edges are curving and intersecting overhead, as they do near North Station, the result may be quite confusing. Yet high overhead edges, which would not be barriers at the ground level, might in the future be very effective orientation elements in a city.

Edges may also, like paths, have directional qualities. The Charles River edge, for example, has the obvious side-from-side differentiation of water and city, and the end-from-end distinction provided by Beacon Hill. Most edges had little of this quality, however.

Figure 24, page 64

It is difficult to think of Chicago without picturing Lake Michigan. It would be interesting to see how many Chicagoans would begin to draw a map of their city by putting down something other than the line of the lake shore. Here is a magnificent example of a visible edge, gigantic in scale, that exposes an entire metropolis to view. Great buildings, parks, and tiny private beaches all come down to the water's edge, which throughout most of its length is accessible and visible to all. The contrast, the differentiation of events along the line, and the lateral breadth are all very strong. The effect is reinforced by the concentration of paths and activities along its extent. The scale is perhaps unrelievedly large and coarse, and too much open space is at times interposed between city and water, as at the Loop. Yet the façade of Chicago on the Lake is an unforgettable sight.

Districts

Districts are the relatively large city areas which the observer can mentally go inside of, and which have some common character. They can be recognized internally, and occasionally can be used as external reference as a person goes by or toward them. Many persons interviewed took care to point out that Boston, while confusing in its path pattern even to the experienced inhabitant, has, in the number and vividness of its differentiated districts, a quality that quite makes up for it. As one person put it:

> Each part of Boston is different from the other. You can tell pretty much what area you're in.

Jersey City has its districts too, but they are primarily ethnic or class districts with little physical distinction. Los Angeles is markedly lacking in strong regions, except for the Civic Center area. The best that can be found are the linear, street-front districts of Skid Row or the financial area. Many Los Angeles subjects referred with some regret to the pleasure of living in a place that has strongly characteristic areas. Said one:

> I like Transportation Row, because it's all there together. That's the main thing; all these other things are spotty . . . There's transportation right there. And all the people have the same thing in common working there. It's very nice.

Subjects, when asked which city they felt to be a well-oriented one, mentioned several, but New York (meaning Manhattan) was unanimously cited. And this city was cited not so much for its grid, which Los Angeles has as well, but because it has a number of well-defined characteristic districts, set in an ordered frame of rivers and streets. Two Los Angeles subjects even referred to Manhattan as being "small" in comparison to their central area! Concepts of size may depend in part on how well a structure can be grasped.

In some Boston interviews, the districts were the basic elements of the city image. One subject, for example, when asked to go from Faneuil Hall to Symphony Hall, replied at once by labeling the trip as going from North End to Back Bay. But even where they were not actively used for orientation, districts were still an important and satisfying part of the experience of living in the city. Recognition of distinct districts in Boston seemed to vary somewhat as acquaintance with the city increased. People most familiar with Boston tended to recognize regions but to rely more heavily for organization and orientation on smaller elements. A few people extremely familiar with Boston were unable to generalize detailed perceptions into districts: conscious of minor differences in all parts of the city, they did not form regional groups of elements.

The physical characteristics that determine districts are thematic continuities which may consist of an endless variety of components: texture, space, form, detail, symbol, building type, use, activity, inhabitants, degree of maintenance, topography. In a closely built city such as Boston, homogeneities of façade—

material, modeling, ornament, color, skyline, especially fenestration—were all basic clues in identifying major districts. Beacon Hill and Commonwealth Avenue are both examples. The clues were not only visual ones: noise was important as well. At times, indeed, confusion itself might be a clue, as it was for the woman who remarked that she knows she is in the North End as soon as she feels she is getting lost.

Figure 55, page 167

Usually, the typical features were imaged and recognized in a characteristic cluster, the thematic unit. The Beacon Hill image, for example, included steep narrow streets; old brick row houses of intimate scale; inset, highly maintained, white doorways; black trim; cobblestones and brick walks; quiet; and upper-class pedestrians. The resulting thematic unit was distinctive by contrast to the rest of the city and could be recognized immediately. In other parts of central Boston, there was some thematic confusion. It was not uncommon to group the Back Bay with the South End, despite their very different use, status, and pattern. This was probably the result of a certain architectural homogeneity, plus some similarity of historical background. Such likenesses tend to blur the city image.

A certain reinforcement of clues is needed to produce a strong image. All too often, there are a few distinctive signs, but not enough for a full thematic unit. Then the region may be recognizable to someone familiar with the city, but it lacks any visual strength or impact. Such, for example, is Little Tokyo in Los Angeles, recognizable by its population and the lettering on its signs but otherwise indistinguishable from the general matrix. Although it is a strong ethnic concentration, probably known to many people, it appeared as only a subsidiary portion of the city image.

Yet social connotations are quite significant in building regions. A series of street interviews indicated the class overtones that many people associate with different districts. Most of the Jersey City regions were class or ethnic areas, discernible only with difficulty for the outsider. Both Jersey City and Boston have shown the exaggerated attention paid to upper-class districts, and the resulting magnification of the importance of elements in those areas. District names also help to give identity to districts even when the thematic unit does not establish a striking contrast with other parts of the city, and traditional associations can play a similar role.

When the main requirement has been satisfied, and a thematic unit that contrasts with the rest of the city has been constituted, the degree of internal homogeneity is less significant, especially if discordant elements occur in a predictable pattern. Small *Figure 57, page 169* stores on street corners establish a rhythm on Beacon Hill that one subject perceived as part of her image. These stores in no way weakened her non-commercial image of Beacon Hill but merely added to it. Subjects could pass over a surprising amount of local disagreement with the characteristic features of a region.

Districts have various kinds of boundaries. Some are hard, definite, precise. Such is the boundary of the Back Bay at the Charles River or at the Public Garden. All agreed on this exact location. Other boundaries may be soft or uncertain, such as the limit between downtown shopping and the office district, to whose existence and approximate location most people would testify. Still other regions have no boundaries at all, as did the South End for many of our subjects. Figure 25 illustrates these

FIG. 25. *Variable boundaries of Boston districts*

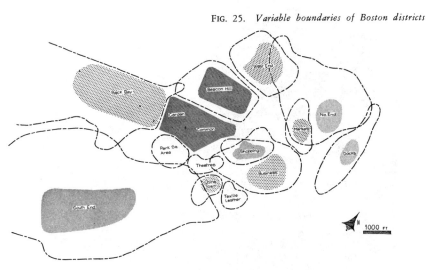

69

Figure 25, page 69

differences of boundary character, in the case of Boston, by outlining both the maximum extent assigned to any district, and the hard core of common agreement.

These edges seem to play a secondary role: they may set limits to a district, and may reinforce its identity, but they apparently have less to do with constituting it. Edges may augment the tendency of districts to fragment the city in a disorganizing way. A few people sensed disorganization as one result of the large number of identifiable districts in Boston: strong edges, by hindering transitions from one district to another, may add to the impression of disorganization.

That type of district which has a strong core, surrounded by a thematic gradient which gradually dwindles away, is not uncommon. Sometimes, indeed, a strong node may create a sort of district in a broader homogeneous zone, simply by "radiation," that is, by the sense of proximity to the nodal point. These are primarily reference areas, with little perceptual content, but they are useful organizing concepts, nevertheless.

FIG. 26. *The market area*

Some well-known Boston districts were unstructured in the public image. The West End and North End were internally undifferentiated for many people who recognized these regions. Even more often, thematically vivid districts such as the market area seemed confusingly shapeless, both externally and internally. The physical sensations of the market activity are unforgettable. Faneuil Hall and its associations reinforce them. Yet the area is shapeless and sprawling, divided by the Central Artery, and hampered by the two activity centers which vie for dominance: Faneuil Hall and Haymarket Square. Dock Square is spatially chaotic. The connections to other areas are either obscure or disrupted by the Artery. Thus the market district simply floated in most images. Instead of fulfilling its potential role as a mosaic link at the head of the Boston peninsula, as does the Common farther down, the district, while distinctive, acted only as a chaotic barrier zone. Beacon Hill, on the other hand, was very highly structured, with internal sub-regions, a node at Louisburg Square, various landmarks, and a configuration of paths.

Figure 26

See Appendix C for a detailed discussion of Beacon Hill

Again, some regions are introvert, turned in upon themselves with little reference to the city outside them, such as Boston's North End or Chinatown. Others may be extrovert, turned outward and connected to surrounding elements. The Common visibly touches neighboring regions, despite its inner path confusions. Bunker Hill in Los Angeles is an interesting example of a district of fairly strong character and historical association, on a very sharp topographical feature lying even closer to the city's heart than does Beacon Hill. Yet the city flows around this element, buries its topographic edges in office buildings, breaks off its path connections, and effectively causes it to fade or even disappear from the city image. Here is a striking opportunity for change in the urban landscape.

Figure 27, page 72

Some districts are single ones, standing alone in their zone. The Jersey City and Los Angeles regions are practically all of this kind, and the South End is a Boston example. Others may be linked together, such as Little Tokyo and the Civic Center in Los Angeles, or West End-Beacon Hill in Boston. In one part of central Boston, inclusive of the Back Bay, the Common, Beacon Hill, the downtown shopping district, and the financial and mar-

ket areas, the regions are close enough together and sufficiently well joined to make a continuous mosaic of distinctive districts. Wherever one proceeds within these limits, one is in a recognizable area. The contrast and proximity of each area, moreover, heightens the thematic strength of each. The quality of Beacon Hill, for example, is sharpened by its nearness to Scollay Square, and to the downtown shopping district.

Nodes

Nodes are the strategic foci into which the observer can enter, typically either junctions of paths, or concentrations of some characteristic. But although conceptually they are small points in the city image, they may in reality be large squares, or somewhat extended linear shapes, or even entire central districts when the city is being considered at a large enough level. Indeed, when conceiving the environment at a national or international level, then the whole city itself may become a node.

The junction, or place of a break in transportation, has compelling importance for the city observer. Because decisions must be made at junctions, people heighten their attention at such places and perceive nearby elements with more than normal clarity. This tendency was confirmed so repeatedly that elements located at junctions may automatically be assumed to derive special prominence from their location. The perceptual importance of such locations shows in another way as well. When subjects were asked where on a habitual trip they first felt a sense of arrival in downtown Boston, a large number of people singled out break-points of transportation as the key places. In a number of cases, the point was at the transition from a highway (Storrow Drive or the Central Artery) to a city street; in another case, the point was at the first railroad stop in Boston (Back Bay Station) even though the subject did not get off there. Inhabitants of Jersey City felt they had left their city when they had passed through the Tonnelle Avenue Circle. The

FIG. 28. *The Charles Street rotary*

transition from one transportation channel to another seems to mark the transition between major structural units. Such points as Scollay Square, the Charles Street rotary, and South Station, are examples of strong junction nodes in Boston. The Charles Street rotary and Scollay Square are both important junction nodes, since both are the switch points at which one

Figure 28, page 73

flanks the obstacle of Beacon Hill. The rotary itself is not a handsome place, but it clearly expresses the transfer between river, bridge, Storrow Drive, Charles Street, and Cambridge Street. Moreover, the open river space, the elevated station, the trains popping in and out of the hillside, the heavy traffic, all can be clearly visualized. The nodes can be important even when the physical form is shapeless and slippery, as it is in

Figure 11, page 28

Journal Square in Jersey City.

The subway stations, strung along their invisible path systems, are strategic junction nodes. Some, like Park Street, Charles Street, Copley, and South Station, were quite important in the Boston map, and a few subjects would organize the rest of the city around them. Most of these key stations were associated with some key surface feature. Others, such as Massachusetts,

Figure 29

were not prominent. This may be because this particular transfer was rarely used by these particular subjects, or because of unfavorable physical circumstances: the lack of visual interest, and the disassociation of the subway node from the street crossing. The stations themselves have many individual characteristics: some are easy to recognize, like Charles Street, others difficult, like Mechanics. Most of them are hard to relate structurally to the ground above them, but some are particularly confusing, such as the utter directionlessness of the upper-level station at Washington Street. A detailed analysis of the imageability of subway systems, or of transit systems in general, would be both useful and fascinating.

Major railroad stations are almost always important city nodes, although their importance may be declining. Boston's South Station was one of the strongest in the city, since it is functionally vital for commuter, subway rider, and intercity traveler, and is visually impressive for its bulk fronting on the open space of Dewey Square. The same might have been said for airports, had our study areas included them. In theory, even ordinary street intersections are nodes, but generally they are not of sufficient prominence to be imaged as more than the incidental crossing of paths. The image cannot carry too many nodal centers.

The other type of node, the thematic concentration, also appeared frequently. Pershing Square in Los Angeles was a *Figure 17, page 36* strong example, being perhaps the sharpest point of the city image, characterized by highly typical space, planting, and activity. Olvera Street and its associated plaza was another case. Boston had quite a number of examples, among them the Jordan-Filene corner and Louisburg Square. The Jordan-Filene corner acts secondarily as a junction between Washington Street and *Figure 30, page 77* Summer Street, and it is associated with a subway stop, but primarily it was recognized as being the very center of the center

FIG. 29. *The nether world of the subway*

of the city. It is the "100 per cent" commercial corner, epitomized to a degree rarely seen in a large American city, but culturally very familiar to Americans. It is a core: the focus and symbol of an important region.

Louisburg Square is another thematic concentration, a well-known quiet residential open space, redolent of the upper-class themes of the Hill, with a highly recognizable fenced park. It

Figure 59, page 171

is a purer example of a concentration than is the Jordan-Filene corner, since it is no transfer point at all, and was only remembered as being "somewhere inside" Beacon Hill. Its importance as a node was out of all proportion to its function.

Nodes may be both junctions and concentrations, as is Jersey City's Journal Square, which is an important bus and automobile transfer and is also a concentration of shopping. Thematic concentrations may be the focus of a region, as is the Jordan-Filene corner, and perhaps Louisburg Square. Others are not foci but are isolated special concentrations, such as Olvera Street in Los Angeles.

A strong physical form is not absolutely essential to the recognition of a node: witness Journal Square and Scollay Square. But where the space has some form, the impact is much stronger. The node becomes memorable. If Scollay Square has a spatial shape commensurate with its functional importance, it would undoubtedly be one of the key features of Boston. In its pres-

Figures 60 and 61, pages 175 and 177

ent form, it could not be remembered in any concrete way. It got such epithets as run-down, or disreputable. Seven out of thirty subjects remembered that it had a subway station; nothing else could be agreed upon. Evidently it made no visual impression, and the connections of various paths to it, which is the basis of its functional importance, were very poorly understood.

A node like Copley Square, on the contrary, which is of less functional importance and has to handle the angled intersection of Huntington Avenue, was very sharply imaged, and the connections of various paths were eminently clear. It was easily identified, principally in terms of its unique individual buildings: the Public Library, Trinity Church, the Copley Plaza Hotel, the sight of the John Hancock Building. It was less of a spatial whole than a concentration of activity and of some uniquely contrasting buildings.

FIG. 30. *Washington and Summer Streets*

Nodes such as Copley Square, Louisburg Square, or Olvera Street, had sharp boundaries, identifiable within a few feet. Others, such as the Jordan-Filene corner, were only the highest peak of some characteristic that had no sharp beginning. In any event, the most successful node seemed both to be unique in some way and at the same time to intensify some surrounding characteristic.

Nodes, like districts, may be introvert or extrovert. Scollay Square is introverted, it gives little directional sense when one is in it or its environs. The principal direction in its surroundings is toward or away from it; the principal locational sensation on arrival is simply "here I am." Boston's Dewey Square, on the other hand, is extroverted. General directions are explained, and connections are clear to the office district, the shopping district, and the waterfront. For one person, South Station in Dewey Square was a huge arrow pointing to the heart of downtown. Approach to such a node seems to come from a particular side. Pershing Square has a similar directional quality, primarily because of the presence of the Biltmore Hotel. In this case, however, exact location in the path grid was uncertain.

Many of these qualities may be summed up by the example of a famous Italian node: the Piazza San Marco in Venice. Highly differentiated, rich and intricate, it stands in sharp contrast to the general character of the city and to the narrow, twisting spaces of its immediate approaches. Yet it ties firmly to the major feature of the city, the Grand Canal, and has an oriented shape that clarifies the direction from which one enters. It is within itself highly differentiated and structured: into two spaces (Piazza and Piazzetta) and with many distinctive landmarks (Duomo, Palazzo Ducale, Campanile, Libreria). Inside, one feels always in clear relation to it, precisely micro-located, as it were. So distinctive is this space that many people who have never been to Venice will recognize its photograph immediately.

Figure 31

Landmarks

Landmarks, the point references considered to be external to the observer, are simple physical elements which may vary widely in scale. There seemed to be a tendency for those more familiar with a city to rely increasingly on systems of landmarks for their guides—to enjoy uniqueness and specialization, in place of the continuities used earlier.

Since the use of landmarks involves the singling out of one element from a host of possibilities, the key physical characteristic of this class is singularity, some aspect that is unique or memorable in the context. Landmarks become more easily identifiable, more likely to be chosen as significant, if they have a clear form; if they contrast with their background; and if there is some

FIG. 31. *The Piazza San Marco, Venice*

prominence of spatial location. Figure-background contrast seems to be the principal factor. The background against which an element stands out need not be limited to immediate surroundings: the grasshopper weathervane of Faneuil Hall, the gold dome of the State House, or the peak of the Los Angeles City Hall are landmarks that are unique against the background of the entire city.

In another sense, subjects might single out landmarks for their cleanliness in a dirty city (the Christian Science buildings in Boston) or for their newness in an old city (the chapel on Arch Street). The Jersey City Medical Center was as well known for its little lawn and flowers as for its great size. The old Hall of Records in the Los Angeles Civic Center is a narrow, dirty structure, set at an angle to the orientation of all the other civic buildings, and with an entirely different scale of fenestration and detail. Despite its minor functional or symbolic importance, this contrast of siting, age, and scale makes it a relatively well-identified image, sometimes pleasant, sometimes irritating. It was several times reported to be "pie-shaped," although it is perfectly rectangular. This is evidently an illusion of the angled siting.

Spatial prominence can establish elements as landmarks in either of two ways: by making the element visible from many locations (the John Hancock Building in Boston, the Richfield Oil Building in Los Angeles), or by setting up a local contrast with nearby elements, i.e., a variation in setback and height. In Los Angeles, on 7th Street at the corner of Flower Street, is an

FIG. 32. *The "little gray lady" on Seventh Street*

old, two-story gray wooden building, set back some ten feet from the building line, containing a few minor shops. This took the attention and fancy of a surprising number of people. One even anthropomorphized it as the "little gray lady." The spatial setback and the intimate scale is a very noticeable and delightful event, in contrast to the great masses that occupy the rest of the frontage.

Figure 32

Location at a junction involving path decisions strengthens a landmark. The Telephone Building at Boston's Bowdoin Square was used, for example, to help people to stay on Cambridge Street. The activity associated with an element may also make it a landmark: an unusual case of this was the Symphony Hall in Los Angeles. This auditorium is the very antithesis of visual imageability: housed in rented quarters in a nondescript building, whose sign simply says "Baptist Temple," it is completely unrecognizable to the stranger. Its strength as a landmark seemed to derive from the contrast and irritation felt between its cultural status and its physical invisibility. Historical associations, or other meanings, are powerful reinforcements, as they are for Faneuil Hall or the State House in Boston. Once a history, a sign, or a meaning attaches to an object, its value as a landmark rises.

Distant landmarks, prominent points visible from many positions, were often well known, but only people unfamiliar with Boston seemed to use them to any great extent in organizing the city and selecting routes for trips. It is the novice who guides himself by reference to the John Hancock Building and the Custom House.

Few people had an accurate sense of where these distant landmarks were and how to make one's way to the base of either building. Most of Boston's distant landmarks, in fact, were "bottomless"; they had a peculiar floating quality. The John Hancock Building, the Custom House, and the Court House are all dominant on the general skyline, but the location and identity of their base is by no means as significant as that of their top.

The gold dome of Boston's State House seems to be one of the few exceptions to this elusiveness. Its unique shape and function, its location at the hill crest and its exposure to the Com-

Figure 58, page 170

mon, the visibility from long distances of its bright gold dome, all make it a key sign for central Boston. It has the satisfying qualities of recognizability at many levels of reference, and of coincidence of symbolic with visual importance.

People who used distant landmarks did so only for very general directional orientation, or, more frequently, in symbolic ways. For one person, the Custom House lent unity to Atlantic Avenue because it can be seen from almost any place on that street. For another, the Custom House set up a rhythm in the financial district, for it can be seen intermittently at many places in that area.

Figure 33

The Duomo of Florence is a prime example of a distant landmark: visible from near and far, by day or night; unmistakable; dominant by size and contour; closely related to the city's traditions; coincident with the religious and transit center; paired with its campanile in such a way that the direction of view can be gauged from a distance. It is difficult to conceive of the city without having this great edifice come to mind.

But local landmarks, visible only in restricted localities, were much more frequently employed in the three cities studied. They

FIG. 33. *The Duomo, Florence*

ran the full range of objects available. The number of local elements that become landmarks appears to depend as much upon how familiar the observer is with his surroundings as upon the elements themselves. Unfamiliar subjects usually mentioned only a few landmarks in office interviews, although they managed to find many more when they went on field trips. Sounds and smells sometimes reinforced visual landmarks, although they did not seem to constitute landmarks by themselves.

Landmarks may be isolated, single events without reinforcement. Except for large or very singular marks, these are weak references, since they are easy to miss and require sustained searching. The single traffic light or street name demands concentration to find. More often, local points were remembered as clusters, in which they reinforced each other by repetition, and were recognizable partly by context.

A sequential series of landmarks, in which one detail calls up anticipation of the next and key details trigger specific moves of the observer, appeared to be a standard way in which these people traveled through the city. In such sequences, there were trigger cues whenever turning decisions must be made and reassuring cues that confirmed the observer in decisions gone by. Additional details often helped to give a sense of nearness to the final destination or to intermediate goals. For emotional security as well as functional efficiency, it is important that such sequences be fairly continuous, with no long gaps, although there may be a thickening of detail at nodes. The sequence facilitates recognition and memorization. Familiar observers can store up a vast quantity of point images in familiar sequences, although recognition may break down when the sequence is reversed or scrambled.

Element Interrelations

These elements are simply the raw material of the environmental image at the city scale. They must be patterned together to provide a satisfying form. The preceding discussions have gone as far as groups of similar elements (nets of paths, clusters of landmarks, mosaics of regions). The next logical step is to consider the interaction of pairs of unlike elements.

Such pairs may reinforce one another, resonate so that they enhance each other's power; or they may conflict and destroy themselves. A great landmark may dwarf and throw out of scale a small region at its base. Properly located, another landmark may fix and strengthen a core; placed off center, it may only mislead, as does the John Hancock Building in relation to Boston's Copley Square. A large street, with its ambiguous character of both edge and path, may penetrate and thus expose a region to view, while at the same time disrupting it. A landmark feature may be so alien to the character of a district as to dissolve the regional continuity, or it may, on the other hand, stand in just the contrast that intensifies that continuity.

Districts in particular, which tend to be of larger size than the other elements, contain within themselves, and are thus related to, various paths, nodes, and landmarks. These other elements not only structure the region internally, they also intensify the identity of the whole by enriching and deepening its character. Beacon Hill in Boston is one example of this effect. In fact, the components of structure and identity (which are the parts of the image in which we are interested) seem to leapfrog as the observer moves up from level to level. The identity of a window may be structured into a pattern of windows, which is the cue for the identification of a building. The buildings themselves are interrelated so as to form an identifiable space, and so on.

Paths, which are dominant in many individual images, and which may be a principal resource in organization at the metropolitan scale, have intimate interrelations with other element types. Junction nodes occur automatically at major intersections and termini, and by their form should reinforce those critical moments in a journey. These nodes, in turn, are not only strengthened by the presence of landmarks (as is Copley Square) but provide a setting which almost guarantees attention for any such mark. The paths, again, are given identity and tempo not only by their own form, or by their nodal junctions, but by the regions they pass through, the edges they move along, and the landmarks distributed along their length.

All these elements operate together, in a context. It would be interesting to study the characteristics of various pairings: landmark-region, node-path, etc. Eventually, one should try to go beyond such pairings to consider total patterns.

Most observers seem to group their elements into intermediate organizations, which might be called complexes. The observer senses the complex as a whole whose parts are interdependent and are relatively fixed in relation to each other. Thus many Bostonians would be able to fit most of the major elements of the Back Bay, the Common, Beacon Hill, and the central shopping, into a single complex. This whole area, in the terms used by Brown[8] in his experiments referred to in Chapter 1, has become one locality. For others, the size of their locality may be much smaller: the central shopping and the near edge of the Common alone, for example. Outside of this complex there are gaps of identity; the observer must run blind to the next whole, even if only momentarily. Although they are close together in physical reality, most people seem to feel only a vague link between Boston's office and financial district and the central shopping district on Washington Street. This peculiar remoteness was also exemplified in the puzzling gap between Scollay Square and Dock Square which are only a block apart. The psychological distance between two localities may be much greater, or more difficult to surmount, than mere physical separation seems to warrant.

Our preoccupation here with parts rather than wholes is a necessary feature of an investigation in a primitive stage. After successful differentiation and understanding of parts, a study can move on to consideration of a total system. There were indications that the image may be a continuous field, the disturbance of one element in some way affecting all others. Even the recognition of an object is as much dependent on context as on the form of the object itself. One major distortion, such as a twisting of the shape of the Common, seemed to be reflected throughout the image of Boston. The disturbance of large-scale construction affected more than its immediate environs. But such field effects have hardly been studied here.

The Shifting Image

Rather than a single comprehensive image for the entire environment, there seemed to be sets of images, which more or less overlapped and interrelated. They were typically arranged in a series of levels, roughly by the scale of area involved, so that the observer moved as necessary from an image at street level to levels of a neighborhood, a city, or a metropolitan region. This arrangement by levels is a necessity in a large and complex environment. Yet it imposes an extra burden of organization on the observer, especially if there is little relation between levels. If a tall building is unmistakable in the city-wide panorama yet unrecognizable from its base, then a chance has been lost to pin together the images at two different levels of organization. The State House on Beacon Hill, on the other hand, seems to pierce through several image levels. It holds a strategic place in the organization of the center.

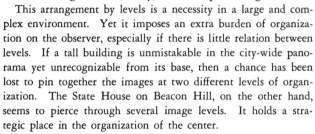

Images may differ not only by the scale of area involved, but by viewpoint, time of day, or season. The image of Faneuil Hall as seen from the markets should be related to its image from a car on the Artery. Washington-Street-by-night should have some continuity, some element of invariance, with Washington-Street-by-day. In order to accomplish this continuity in the face of sensuous confusion, many observers drained their images of visual content, using abstractions such as "restaurant" or "second street." These will operate both day and night, driving or walking, rain or shine, albeit with some effort and loss.

The observer must also adjust his image to secular shifts in the physical reality around him. Los Angeles illustrated the practical and emotional strains induced as the image is confronted with constant physical changes. It would be important to know how to maintain continuity through these changes. Just as ties are needed between level and level of organization, so are continuities required which persist through a major change. This might be facilitated by the retention of an old tree, a path trace, or some regional character.

The sequence in which sketch maps were drawn seemed to indicate that the image develops, or grows, in different ways. This may perhaps have some relation to the way in which it first develops as an individual becomes familiar with his environment. Several types were apparent:

a. Quite frequently, images were developed along, and then outward from, familiar lines of movement. Thus a map might be drawn as branching out from a point of entrance, or beginning from some base line such as Massachusetts Avenue.

b. Other maps were begun by the construction of an enclosing outline, such as the Boston peninsula, which was then filled in toward the center.

c. Still others, particularly in Los Angeles, began by laying down a basic repeating pattern (the path gridiron) and then adding detail.

d. Somewhat fewer maps started as a set of adjacent regions, which were then detailed as to connections and interiors.

e. A few Boston examples developed from a familiar kernel, a dense familiar element on which everything was ultimately hung.

The image itself was not a precise, miniaturized model of reality, reduced in scale and consistently abstracted. As a purposive simplification, it was made by reducing, eliminating, or even adding elements to reality, by fusion and distortion, by relating and structuring the parts. It was sufficient, perhaps better, for its purpose if rearranged, distorted, "illogical." It resembled that famous cartoon of the New Yorker's view of the United States.

However distorted, there was a strong element of topological invariance with respect to reality. It was as if the map were drawn on an infinitely flexible rubber sheet; directions were twisted, distances stretched or compressed, large forms so changed from their accurate scale projection as to be at first unrecognizable. But the sequence was usually correct, the map was rarely torn and sewn back together in another order. This continuity is necessary if the image is to be of any value.

Image Quality

Study of various individual images among the Bostonians revealed certain other distinctions between them. For example, images of an element differed between observers in terms of their relative density, i.e., the extent to which they were packed with detail. They might be relatively dense, as a picture of Newbury Street which identifies each building along its length, or relatively thin, when Newbury Street is characterized simply as a street bordered by old houses of mixed use.

Another distinction could be made between concrete, sensuously vivid images, and those which were highly abstract, generalized, and void of sensuous content. Thus the mental picture of a building might be vivid, involving its shape, color, texture, and detail, or be relatively abstract, the structure being identified as "a restaurant" or the "third building from the corner."

Vivid does not necessarily equate with dense, nor thin with abstract. An image might be both dense and abstract, as in the case of the taxicab dispatcher's knowledge of a city street, which related house numbers to uses along block after block, yet could not describe those buildings in any concrete sense.

Images could be further distinguished according to their structural quality: the manner in which their parts were arranged and interrelated. There were four stages along a continuum of increasing structural precision:

a. The various elements were free; there was no structure or interrelation between parts. We found no pure cases of this type, but several images were definitely disjointed, with vast gaps and many unrelated elements. Here rational movement was impossible without outside help, unless a systematic coverage of the entire area were to be resorted to (which meant the building up of a new structure on the spot).

b. In others, the structure became positional; the parts were roughly related in terms of their general direction and perhaps even relative distance from each other, while still remaining disconnected. One subject in particular always related herself to a few elements, without knowing definite connections between them. Movement was accomplished by searching, by moving out in the correct general direction, while weaving back and forth to cover a band and having an estimate of distance to correct overshooting.

c. Most often, perhaps, the structure was flexible; parts were connected one to the other, but in a loose and flexible manner, as if by limp or elastic ties. The sequence of events was known, but the mental map might be quite distorted, and its distortion might shift at different moments. To quote one subject: "I like to think of a few focal points and how to get from one to another, and the rest I don't bother to learn." With a flexible structure, movement was easier, since it proceeded along known paths, through known sequences. Motion between pairs of elements not habitually connected, or along other than habitual paths, might still be very confusing, however.

d. As connections multiplied, the structure tended to become rigid; parts were firmly interconnected in all dimensions; and any distortions became built in. The possessor of such a map can move much more freely, and can interconnect new points at will. As the density of the image builds up, it begins to take on the characteristics of a total field, in which interaction is possible in any direction and at any distance.

These characteristics of structure might apply in different ways at different levels. For example, two city regions may each possess rigid internal structures, and both connect at some seam or node. But this connection may fail to interlock with the internal structures, so that the connection itself is simply flexible. This effect seemed to occur for many Bostonians at Scollay Square, for example.

Total structure may also be distinguished in a still different way. For some, their images were organized rather instantaneously, as a series of wholes and parts descending from the general to the particular. This organization had the quality of a static map. Connection was made by moving up to the necessary bridging generality, and back down to the desired particular. To go from City Hospital .to the Old North Church, for example, one might first consider that the hospital was in the South End and that the South End was in 'central Boston, then locate the North End in Boston and the church within the North End. This type of image might be called hierarchical.

For others, the image was put together in a more dynamic way, parts being interconnected by a sequence over time (even if the time was quite brief), and pictured as though seen by a motion picture camera. It was more closely related to the actual experience of moving through the city. This might be called a continuous organization, employing unrolling interconnections instead of static hierarchies.

One might infer from this that the images of greatest value are those which most closely approach a strong total field: dense, rigid, and vivid; which make use of all element types and form characteristics without narrow concentration; and which can be put together either hierarchically or continuously, as occasion demands. We may find, of course, that such an image is rare or impossible, that there are strong individual or cultural types which cannot transcend their basic abilities. In this case, an environment should be geared to the appropriate cultural type, or shaped in many ways so as to satisfy the varying demands of the individuals who inhabit it.

We are continuously engaged in the attempt to organize our surroundings, to structure and identify them. Various environments are more or less amenable to such treatment. When reshaping cities it should be possible to give them a form which facilitates these organizing efforts rather than frustrates them.

IV.

CITY FORM

We have the opportunity of forming our new city world into an imageable landscape: visible, coherent, and clear. It will require a new attitude on the part of the city dweller, and a physical reshaping of his domain into forms which entrance the eye, which organize themselves from level to level in time and space, which can stand as symbols for urban life. The present study yields some clues in this respect.

Most objects which we are accustomed to call beautiful, such as a painting or a tree, are single-purpose things, in which, through long development or the impress of one will, there is an intimate, visible linkage from fine detail to total structure. A city is a multi-purpose, shifting organization, a tent for many functions, raised by many hands and with relative speed. Complete specialization, final meshing, is improbable and undesirable. The form must be somewhat noncommittal, plastic to the purposes and perceptions of its citizens.

Yet there are fundamental functions of which the city forms may be expressive: circulation, major land-uses, key focal points.

The common hopes and pleasures, the sense of community may be made flesh. Above all, if the environment is visibly organized and sharply identified, then the citizen can inform it with his own meanings and connections. Then it will become a true *place*, remarkable and unmistakable.

To take a single example, Florence is a city of powerful character which has deep hold on the affection of many people. Although many foreigners will at first react to it as cold or forbidding, yet they cannot deny its special intensity. To live in this environment, whatever the economic or social problems encountered, seems to add an extra depth to experience, whether of delight or of melancholy or of belonging.

The city of course has an economic, cultural, and political history of staggering proportions, and the visual evidence of this past accounts for much of the strong Florentine character. But it is also a highly visible city. It lies in a bowl of hills along the Arno River, so that the hills and the city are almost always intervisible. On the south, the open country penetrates almost to the heart of the city, setting up a clear contrast, and from one of the last steep hills a terrace gives an "overhead" view of the urban core. On the north, small distinct settlements, such as Fiesole and Settignano, are perched visibly on characteristic hills. From the precise symbolic and transportation center of the city rises the huge and unmistakable dome of the Duomo, flanked by Giotto's campanile, a point of orientation visible in every section of the city and for miles outside of it. This dome is the symbol of Florence.

Figure 34

Figure 33, page 82

The central city has district characters of almost oppressive strength: slot-like streets, stone-paved; tall stone and stucco buildings, yellowish-gray in color, with shutters, iron grilles, and cave-like entrances, topped by the characteristic deep Florentine eaves. Within this area are many strong nodes, whose distinctive forms are reinforced by their special use or class of user. The central area- is studded with landmarks, each with its own name and story. The Arno River cuts through the whole and connects it to the larger landscape.

To these clear and differentiated forms people have made strong attachments, whether of past history or of their own ex-

FIG. 34. *Florence from the south*

perience. Every scene is instantly recognizable, and brings to mind a flood of associations. Part fits into part. The visual environment becomes an integral piece of its inhabitants' lives. The city is by no means perfect, even in the limited sense of imageability; nor does all of the city's visual success lie in this one quality. But there seems to be a simple and automatic pleasure, a feeling of satisfaction, presence, and rightness, which arises from the mere sight of the city, or the chance to walk through its streets.

Florence is an unusual city. Indeed, even if we no longer confine ourselves to the United States, the highly visible city is still somewhat of a rarity. Imageable villages or city sections are legion, but there may be no more than twenty or thirty cities in the world which present a consistently strong image. Even so, not one of these would encompass more than a few square miles of area. Although the metropolis is no longer a rare phenomenon, yet nowhere in the world is there a metropolitan area with any strong visual character, any evident structure. The famous cities all suffer from the same faceless sprawl at the periphery.

One may reasonably ask, then, if a consistently imageable metropolis (or even a city), is in fact possible; and whether it would be appreciated if it did exist. Given the lack of examples, it is necessary to argue largely on supposition and by the projection of past events. Men have increased the scope of their perception before, when faced with a new challenge, and there is little reason to see why it could not happen again. There are, furthermore, existing highway sequences which indicate that such a new large-scale organization might be possible.

It is also possible to cite examples of visible form at this larger scale which are not urban examples. Most people can call to mind a few favorite landscapes which have this differentiation, this structure and clear shape that we would like to produce in our living environments. The landscape south of Florence, on the road to Poggibonsi, has this character for mile after mile. The valleys, ridges, and little hills are of great variety, but lead down in a common system. The Appenines bound the horizon in the north and east. The ground, visible over long distances, is cleared and intensively cultivated for a great variety of crops—wheat, olive, grape—each clearly discernible for its own particular color and form. Each fold of the ground is mirrored in the lay of the fields, plants, and paths; each hillock is crowned by some little settlement, church, or tower, so that one could say: "Here is my town, and there is that other." Guided by the geological structure of the natural features, men have achieved a delicate and visible adjustment of their actions. The whole is one landscape, and yet each part can be distinguished from its neighbor.

Sandwich, New Hampshire, might be taken as another example, where the White Mountains sink down into the rolling headwaters of the Merrimac and the Piscataqua Rivers. The forested mountain wall is sharply contrasted with the rolling, half-cultivated country below. To the south the Ossipee Mountains are a final isolated upthrust of hills. Several of the peaks, such as Mt. Chocorua, are of peculiar individual form. The effect is strongest in the "intervales," the flat plateaus at the very base of the mountains, which are entirely cleared and which have that strange and powerful sensation of special "place," exactly comparable to the sensation of strong locale in a city like Florence. At the time when all the lower ground was cleared for farming, the entire landscape must have had this quality.

Hawaii might be taken as another more exotic example: with its sharp mountains, highly colored rocks and great cliffs, luxuriant and highly individualized vegetation, contrast of sea and land, and dramatic transitions between one side of the island and another.

These are, of course, personal examples; the reader can substitute his own. Occasionally they are the product of powerful natural events such as on Hawaii; more often, as in Tuscany, they are the product of human modification working for consistent purposes and with common technology on the basic structure provided by a continuous geologic process. If successful, this modification is done with an awareness of the interconnectedness, and yet the individuality, of both natural resources and human purposes.

As an artificial world, the city should be so in the best sense: made by art, shaped for human purposes. It is our ancient habit to adjust to our environment, to discriminate and organize perceptually whatever is present to our senses. Survival and dominance based themselves on this sensuous adaptability, yet now we may go on to a new phase of this interaction. On home grounds, we may begin to adapt the environment itself to the perceptual pattern and symbolic process of the human being.

Designing the Paths

To heighten the imageability of the urban environment is to facilitate its visual identification and structuring. The elements isolated above—the paths, edges, landmarks, nodes, and regions— are the building blocks in the process of making firm, differentiated structures at the urban scale. What hints can we draw from the preceding material as to the characteristics such elements might have in a truly imageable environment?

The paths, the network of habitual or potential lines of movement through the urban complex, are the most potent means by which the whole can be ordered. The key lines should have some singular quality which marks them off from the surrounding channels: a concentration of some special use or activity along their margins, a characteristic spatial quality, a special texture of floor or façade, a particular lighting pattern, a unique set of smells or sounds, a typical detail or mode of planting. Washington Street may be known by its intensive commerce and slot-like space; Commonwealth Avenue by its tree-lined center.

These characters should be so applied as to give continuity to the path. If one or more of these qualities is employed consistently along the line, then the path may be imaged as a continuous, unified element. It may be a boulevard planting of trees, a singular color or texture of pavement, or the classical continuity of bordering façades. The regularity may be a rhythmic one, a repetition of space openings, monuments, or corner drugstores. The very concentration of habitual travel along a path, as by a transit line, will reinforce this familiar, continuous image.

This leads to what might be called a visual hierarchy of the streets and ways, analogous to the familiar recommendation of a functional hierarchy: a sensuous singling out of the key channels, and their unification as continuous perceptual elements. This is the skeleton of the city image.

The line of motion should have clarity of direction. The human computer is disturbed by long successions of turnings, or by gradual, ambiguous curves which in the end produce major directional shifts. The continuous twistings of Venetian calli or of the streets in one of Olmsted's romantic plans, or the gradual turning of Boston's Atlantic Avenue, soon confuse all but the most highly adapted observers. A straight path has clear direction, of course, but so does one with a few well-defined turns close to 90 degrees, or another of many slight turns which yet never loses its basic direction.

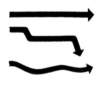

Observers seem to endow a path with a sense of pointing or irreversible direction, and to identify a street with the destination toward which it goes. A street is perceived, in fact, as a thing which goes toward something. The path should support this perceptually by strong termini, and by a gradient or a directional differentiation, so that it is given a sense of progression, and the opposite directions are unlike. A common gradient is that of ground slope, and one is regularly instructed to go "up" or "down" a street, but there are many others. A progressive thickening of signs, stores, or people may mark the approach to a shopping node; there can be a gradient of color or texture of planting as well; a shortening of block length or a funneling of space may signal the nearness of the city center. Asymmetries may also be used. Perhaps one can proceed by "keeping the park on the left," or by moving "toward the golden dome." Arrows can be used, or all projecting surfaces facing one direction might have a coded color. All these means make the path an oriented element to which other things can be referred. There is no danger of making a "wrong-way" mistake.

If positions along the line can be differentiated in some measurable way, then the line is not only oriented, but scaled as well. Ordinary house numbering is such a technique. A less abstract means is the marking of an identifiable point on the line, so that other places may be thought of as "before" or "after." Several check points improve the definition. Or a quality (such as the space of the corridor) may have a modulation of gradient at a changing rate, so that the change itself has a recognizable form. Thus one could say that a certain place is "just before the street narrows down very rapidly," or "on the shoulder of the hill before the final ascent." The mover can feel not only "I am going in the right direction," but "I am almost there" as well. Where the journey contains such a series of distinct events, a reaching and passing of one sub-goal after another, the trip itself takes on meaning and becomes an experience in its own right.

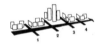

Observers are impressed, even in memory, by the apparent "kinesthetic" quality of a path, the sense of motion along it: turning, rising, falling. Particularly is this true where the path is traversed at high speed. A great descending curve which approaches a city center can produce an unforgettable

image. Tactile and inertial senses enter into this perception of motion, but vision seems to be dominant. Objects along the path can be arranged to sharpen the effect of motion parallax or perspective, or the course of the path ahead may be made visible. The dynamic shaping of the movement line will give it identity and will produce a continuous experience over time.

Any visual exposure of the path, or its goal, heightens its image. A great bridge may do this, an axial avenue, a concave profile, or the distant silhouette of the final destination. The presence of the path may be made evident by high landmarks along it, or other hints. The vital line of circulation becomes palpable before our eyes, and can become the symbol of a fundamental urban function. Conversely, the experience is heightened if the path reveals the presence of other city elements to the traveler: if it penetrates or strikes them tangentially, if it offers hints and symbols of what is passed by. A subway, for example, instead of being buried alive, might suddenly pass through the shopping zone itself, or its station might recall by its form the nature of the city above it. The path might be so shaped that the flow itself becomes sensuously evident: split lanes, ramps, and spirals would allow the traffic to indulge in self-contemplation. All these are techniques of increasing the visual scope of the traveler.

Normally, a city is structured by an organized set of paths. The strategic point in such a set is the intersection, the point of connection and decision for the man in motion. If this can be visualized clearly, if the intersection itself makes a vivid image and if the lie of the two paths with respect to each other is clearly expressed, then the observer can build a satisfactory structure. Boston's Park Square is an ambiguous joining of major surface streets; the junction of Arlington Street and Commonwealth Avenue is clear and sharp. Universally, subway stations fail to make such clear visual joints. Special care must be taken to explain the intricate intersections of modern path systems.

A joint of more than two paths is normally quite difficult to conceptualize. A structure of paths must have a certain simplicity of form to make a clear image. Simplicity in a topological rather than a geometrical sense is required, so that an irregular but approximately right-angled crossing is preferable to a precise trisection. Examples of such simple structures are parallel sets or spindle forms; one-, two-, or three-barred crosses; rectangles; or a few axes linked together.

Paths may also be imaged, not as a specific pattern of certain individual elements, but rather as a network which explains the typical relations between all paths in the set without identifying any particular path. This condition implies a grid which has some consistency, whether of direction, topological interrelation, or interspacing. A pure gridiron combines all three, but directional or topological invariance may by themselves be quite effective. The image sharpens if all paths running in one topological sense, or compass direction, are visually differentiated from the other paths. Thus the spatial distinction between Manhattan's streets and avenues is effective. Color, planting, or detail might serve equally well. Naming and numbering, gradients of space, topography, or detail, differentiation within the net may all give the grid a progressive or even a scaled sense.

There is a final way of organizing a path or a set of paths, which will become of increasing importance in a world of great distances and high speeds. It might be called "melodic" in analogy to music. The events and characteristics along the path—landmarks, space changes, dynamic sensations—might be organized as a melodic line, perceived and imaged as a form which is experienced over a substantial time interval. Since the image would be of a total melody rather than a series of separate points, that image could presumably be more inclusive, and yet less demanding. The form might be the classical introduction-development-climax-conclusion sequence, or it might take more subtle shapes, such as those which avoid final conclusions. The approach to San Francisco across the bay hints at a type of this melodic organization. The technique offers a rich field for design development and experiment.

Design of Other Elements

Edges as well as paths call for a certain continuity of form throughout their length. The edge of a business district, for example, may be an important concept, but be difficult to discover in the field because it has no recognizable continuity of form. The edge also gains strength if it is laterally visible for some distance, marks a sharp gradient of area character, and clearly joins the two bounded regions. Thus the abrupt cessation of a medieval city at its wall, the fronting of skyscraper apartments on Central Park, the clear transition from water to land at a sea-front, all are powerful visual impressions. When two strongly contrasting regions are set in close juxtaposition, and their meeting edge is laid open to view, then visual attention is easily concentrated.

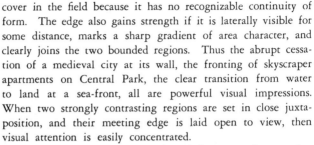

Particularly where the regions bounded are not of contrasting nature, then it is useful to differentiate the two sides of an edge, to orient the observer in the "inside-outside" sense. It may be accomplished by contrasting materials, by a consistent concavity of line, or by planting. Or the edge may be shaped to give orientation along its length, by a gradient, by identifiable points at intervals, or by individualizing one end with respect to the other. When the edge is not continuous and self-closing, then it is important that its ends have definite termini, recognizable anchors which complete and locate the line. The image of the Boston waterfront, which is usually not mentally continuous with the Charles River line, lacks a perceptual anchor at either end, and is in consequence an indecisive and ⁻fuzzy element in the total Boston image.

An edge may be more than simply a dominant barrier if some visual or motion penetration is allowed through it—if it is, as it were, structured to some depth with the regions on either side. It then becomes a seam rather than a barrier, a line of exchange along which two areas are sewn together.

If an important edge is provided with many visual and circulation connections to the rest of the city structure, then it becomes a feature to which everything else is easily aligned. One way of increasing the visibility of an edge is by increasing its accessibility or use, as when opening a waterfront to traffic or recreation. Another might be to construct high overhead edges, visible for long distances.

The essential characteristic of a viable landmark, on the other hand, is its singularity, its contrast with its context or background. It may be a tower silhouetted over low roofs, flowers against a stone wall, a bright surface in a drab street, a church among stores, a projection in a continuous façade. Spatial prominence is particularly compelling of attention. Control of the landmark and its context may be needed: the restriction of signs to specified surfaces, height limits which apply to all but one building. The object is also more remarkable if it has a clarity of general form, as does a column or a sphere. If in addition it has some richness of detail or texture, it will surely invite the eye.

A landmark is not necessarily a large object; it may be a doorknob as well as a dome. Its location is crucial: if large or tall, the spatial setting must allow it to be seen; if small, there are certain zones that receive more perceptual attention than others: floor surfaces, or nearby façades at, or slightly below, eye-level. Any breaks in transportation—nodes, decision points— are places of intensified perception. Interviews show that ordinary buildings at route decision points are remembered clearly, while distinctive structures along a continuous route may have slipped into obscurity. A landmark is yet stronger if visible over an extended range of time or distance, more useful if the direction of view can be distinguished. If identifiable from near and far, while moving rapidly or slowly, by night or day, it then becomes a stable anchor for the perception of the complex and shifting urban world.

Image strength rises when the landmark coincides with a concentration of association. If the distinctive building is the scene of an historic event, or if the bright-colored door is your own, then it becomes a landmark indeed. Even the bestowal of a name has power, once that name is generally known and accepted. Indeed, if we are to make our environment meaningful, such a coincidence of association and imageability is necessary.

Single landmarks, unless they are dominant ones, are likely to be weak references by themselves. Their recognition requires sustained attention. If they are clustered, however, they reinforce each other in a more than additive way. Familiar observers develop landmark clusters out of most unpromising

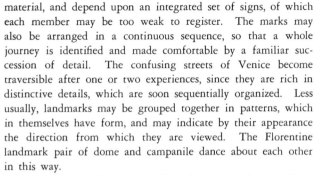

material, and depend upon an integrated set of signs, of which each member may be too weak to register. The marks may also be arranged in a continuous sequence, so that a whole journey is identified and made comfortable by a familiar succession of detail. The confusing streets of Venice become traversible after one or two experiences, since they are rich in distinctive details, which are soon sequentially organized. Less

usually, landmarks may be grouped together in patterns, which in themselves have form, and may indicate by their appearance the direction from which they are viewed. The Florentine landmark pair of dome and campanile dance about each other in this way.

The nodes are the conceptual anchor points in our cities. Rarely in the United States, however, do they have a form adequate to support this attention, other than a certain concentration of activity.

The first prerequisite for such perceptual support is the achievement of identity by the singular and continuous quality of the walls, floor, detail, lighting, vegetation, topography, or skyline of the node. The essence of this type of element is that it be a distinct, unforgettable *place,* not to be confused with any other. Intensity of use strengthens this identity, of course, and sometimes the very intensity of use creates visual shapes which are distinctive, as in Times Square. But our shopping centers and transport breaks which lack this visual character are legion.

The node is more defined if it has a sharp, closed boundary, and does not trail off uncertainly on every side; more remarkable if. provided with one or two objects which are foci of attention. . But if it can have coherent spatial form, it will be irresistible. This is the classic concept of forming static outdoor spaces, and there are many techniques for the expression and definition of such a space: transparencies, overlappings, light modulation, perspective, surface gradients, closure, articulation, patterns of motion and sound.

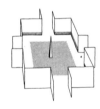

If a break in transportation or a decision point on a path can be made to coincide with the node, the node will receive even more attention. The joint between path and node must be visible and expressive, as it is in the case of intersecting paths. The traveler must see how he enters the node, where the break occurs, and how he goes outward.

These condensation points can, by radiation, organize large districts around themselves if their presence is somehow signalized in the surroundings. A gradient of use or other characteristic may lead up to the node, or its space may occasionally be visible from outside; or it may contain high landmarks. The city of Florence focuses in this manner around its Duomo and Palazzo Vecchio, both standing in major nodes. The node may emit characteristic light or sound, or its presence be hinted at by symbolic detail in the hinterland, which echoes some quality of the node itself. Sycamores in a district might reveal the proximity of a square noted for a heavy plantation of these trees, or cobblestone pavements lead up to a cobbled enclosure.

If the node has a local orientation within itself—an "up" or "down," a "left" or a "right," a "front" or a "back"—then it can be related to the larger orientation system. When recognized paths enter in a clear joint, then the tie can also be made. In either case, the observer feels the presence of the city structure around him. He knows in what direction to move outward to reach a goal, and the particularity of the place itself is enhanced by the felt contrast with the total image.

It is possible to arrange a series of nodes to form a related structure. They can be linked together by close juxtaposition or by allowing them to be intervisible, as are the Piazze S. Marco and SS. Annunziata in Florence. They may be put in some common relation to a path or edge, joined by a short linking element, or related by an echo of some characteristic from one to the other. Such linkages can structure substantial city regions.

A city district in its simplest sense is an area of homogeneous character, recognized by clues which are continuous throughout the district and discontinuous elsewhere. The homogeneity may be of spatial characteristics, like the narrow sloping streets of Beacon Hill; of building type, like the swell-front row houses of the South End; of style or of topography. It may be a typical building feature, like the white stoops of Baltimore. It may be a continuity of color, texture, or material, of floor surface,

scale or façade detail, lighting, planting, or silhouette. The more these characters overlap, the stronger the impression of a unified region. It appears that a "thematic unit" of three or four such characters is particularly useful in delimiting an area. Persons interviewed usually held together in their minds a small cluster of such characters: such as the narrow sloping streets, brick pavements, small-scale row houses, and recessed doorways of Beacon Hill. Several such characters can be held fixed in a district, while other factors are varied as desired.

Where physical homogeneity coincides with use and status, the effect is unmistakable. The visual character of Beacon Hill is directly reinforced by its status as upper-class residence. The more usual American case is the reverse: use-character receives little support from visual character.

A district is further sharpened by the definiteness and closure of its boundary. A Boston housing project on Columbia Point has an island-like character which may be undesirable socially but is perceptually quite clear. Any small island, in fact, has a charming particularity for this reason. And if the region is easily visible as a whole, as by high or panoramic views, or by the convexity or concavity of its site, then its separateness is sealed.

The district may be structured within itself as well. There may be sub-districts, internally differentiated while conforming to the whole; nodes which radiate structure by gradients or other hints; patterns of internal paths. The Back Bay is structured by its network of alphabetized paths, and usually appears clearly, unmistakably, and somewhat enlarged on most sketch maps. A structured region is likely to be a more vivid image. Furthermore, it tells its inhabitants not simply "you are somewhere in X," but "you are in X, near Y."

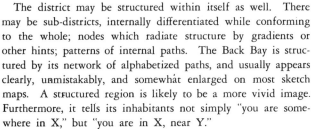

When suitably differentiated within, a district can express connections with other city features. The boundary must now be penetrable: a seam, not a barrier. District may join to district, by juxtaposition, intervisibility, relation to a line, or by some link such as a mediating node, path or small district. Beacon Hill is linked to the metropolitan core by the spatial region of the Common, and therein lies much of its attraction.

Such links heighten the character of each district, and bring together great urban areas.

It is conceivable that we might have a region which is not simply characterized by homogeneous spatial quality, but is in fact a true spatial region, a structured continuum of spatial form. In a primitive sense, such large urban spaces as river openings are of this nature. A spatial region would be distinguished from a spatial node (a square) because it could not be scanned quickly. It could only be experienced, as a patterned play of spatial changes, by a rather protracted journey through it. Perhaps the processional courts of Peking, or the canal spaces of Amsterdam, have this quality. Presumably they evoke an image of great power.

Form Qualities

These clues for urban design can be summarized in another way, since there are common themes that run through the whole set: the repeated references to certain general physical characteristics. These are the categories of direct interest in design, since they describe qualities that a designer may operate upon. They might be summarized as follows:

1. *Singularity* or figure-background clarity: sharpness of boundary (as an abrupt cessation of city development); closure (as an enclosed square); contrast of surface, form, intensity, complexity, size, use, spatial location (as a single tower, a rich decoration, a glaring sign). The contrast may be to the immediate visible surroundings, or to the observer's experience. These are the qualities that identify an element, make it remarkable, noticeable, vivid, recognizable. Observers, as their familiarity increases, seem to depend less and less on gross physical continuities to organize the whole, and to delight more and more in contrast and uniqueness which vivify the scene.

2. *Form Simplicity:* clarity and simplicity of visible form in the geometrical sense, limitation of parts (as the clarity of a grid system, a rectangle, a dome). Forms of this nature are much more easily incorporated in the image, and there is evidence that observers will distort complex facts to simple forms, even

at some perceptual and practical cost. When an element is not simultaneously visible as a whole, its shape may be a topological distortion of a simple form and yet be quite understandable.

3. *Continuity:* continuance of edge or surface (as in a street channel, skyline, or setback); nearness of parts (as a cluster of buildings); repetition of rhythmic interval (as a street-corner pattern); similarity, analogy, or harmony of surface, form, or use (as in a common building material, repetitive pattern of bay windows, similarity of market activity, use of common signs). These are the qualities that facilitate the perception of a complex physical reality as one or as interrelated, the qualities which suggest the bestowing of single identity.

4. *Dominance:* dominance of one part over others by means of size, intensity, or interest, resulting in the reading of the whole as a principal feature with an associated cluster (as in the "Harvard Square area"). This quality, like continuity, allows the necessary simplification of the image by omission and subsumption. Physical characteristics, to the extent that they are over the threshold of attention at all, seem to radiate their image conceptually to some degree, spreading out from a center.

5. *Clarity of Joint:* high visibility of joints and seams (as at a major intersection, or on a sea-front); clear relation and interconnection (as of a building to its site, or of a subway station to the street above). These joints are the strategic moments of structure and should be highly perceptible.

6. *Directional Differentiation:* asymmetries, gradients, and radial references which differentiate one end from another (as on a path ·going uphill, away from the sea, and toward the center); or one side from another (as with buildings fronting a park); or one compass direction from another (as by the sunlight, or by the width of north-south avenues). These qualities are heavily used in structuring on the larger scale.

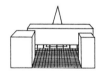

7. *Visual Scope:* qualities which increase the range and penetration of vision, either actually or symbolically. These include transparencies (as with glass or buildings on stilts); overlaps (as when structures appear behind others); vistas and panoramas which increase the depth of vision (as on axial streets, broad open spaces, high views); articulating elements (foci, measuring

rods, penetrating objects) which visually explain a space; concavity (as of a background hill or curving street) which exposes farther objects to view; clues which speak of an element otherwise invisible (as the sight of activity which is characteristic of a region to come, or the use of characteristic detail to hint at the proximity of another element). All these related qualities facilitate the grasping of a vast and complex whole by increasing, as it were, the efficiency of vision: its range, penetration, and resolving power.

8. *Motion Awareness:* the qualities which make sensible to the observer, through both the visual and the kinesthetic senses, his own actual or potential motion.   Such are the devices which improve the clarity of slopes, curves, and interpenetrations; give the experience of motion parallax and perspective; maintain the consistency of direction or direction change; or make visible the distance interval.   Since a city is sensed in motion, these qualities are fundamental, and they are used to structure and even to identify, wherever they are coherent enough to make it possible (as: "go left, then right," "at the sharp bend," or "three blocks along this street").   These qualities reinforce and develop what an observer can do to interpret direction or distance, and to sense form in motion itself.   With increasing speed, these techniques will need further development in the modern city.

9. *Time Series:* series which are sensed over time, including both simple item-by-item linkages, where one element is simply knitted to the two elements before and behind it (as in a casual sequence of detailed landmarks), and also series which are truly structured in time and thus melodic in nature (as if the landmarks would increase in intensity of form until a climax point were reached).   The former (simple sequence) is very commonly used, particularly along familiar paths.   Its melodic counterpart is more rarely seen, but may be most important to develop in the large, dynamic, modern metropolis.   Here what would be imaged would be the developing pattern of elements, rather than the elements themselves—just as we remember melodies, not notes.   In a complex environment, it might even be possible to use contrapuntal techniques: moving patterns of opposing melodies or rhythms.   These are sophisticated methods,

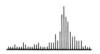

and must be consciously developed. We need fresh thought on the theory of forms which are perceived as a continuity over time, as well as on design archetypes which exhibit a melodic sequence of image elements or a formed succession of space, texture, motion, light, or silhouette.

10. *Names and Meanings:* non-physical characteristics which may enhance the imageability of an element. Names, for example, are important in crystallizing identity. They occasionally give locational clues (North Station). Naming systems (as in the alphabetizing of a street series), will also facilitate the structuring of elements. Meanings and associations, whether social, historical, functional, economic, or individual, constitute an entire realm lying beyond the physical qualities we deal with here. They strongly reinforce such suggestions toward identity or structure as may be latent in the physical form itself.

All of the above-mentioned qualities do not work in isolation. Where one quality is present alone (as a continuity of building material with no other common feature), or the qualities are in conflict (as in two areas of common building type but of different function), the total effect may be weak, or require effort to identify and structure. A certain amount of repetition, redundancy, and reinforcement seems to be necessary. Thus a region would be unmistakable which had a simple form, a continuity of building type and use, which was singular in the city, sharply bounded, clearly jointed to a neighboring region, and visually concave.

The Sense of the Whole

In discussing design by element types, there is a tendency to skim over the interrelation of the parts into a whole. In such a whole, paths would expose and prepare for the districts, and link together the various nodes. The nodes would joint and mark off the paths, while the edges would bound off the districts, and the landmarks would indicate their cores. It is the total orchestration of these units which would knit together a dense and vivid image, and sustain it over areas of metropolitan scale.

The five elements—path, edge, district, node, and landmark—must be considered simply as convenient empirical categories, within and around which it has been possible to group a mass of information. To the extent that they are useful, they will act as building blocks for the designer. Having mastered their characteristics, he will have the task of organizing a whole which will be sensed sequentially, whose parts will be perceived only in context. Were he to arrange a sequence of ten landmarks along a path, then one of these marks would have an utterly different image quality than if it were placed singly and prominently at the city core.

Forms should be manipulated so that there is a strand of continuity between the multiple images of a big city: day and night, winter and summer, near and far, static and moving, attentive and absent-minded. Major landmarks, regions, nodes, or paths should be recognizable under diverse conditions, and yet in a concrete, rather than an abstract way. This is not to say that the image should be the same in each case. But if Louisburg Square in the snow has a shape that matches Louisburg Square in midsummer, or if the State House dome by night shines in a way that recalls that dome seen in the day, then the contrasting quality of each image becomes even more sharply savored because of the common tie. One is now able to hold together two quite different city views, and thus to encompass the scale of the city in a way otherwise impossible: to approach the ideal of an image which is a total field.

While the complexity of the modern city calls for continuity, it also furnishes a great delight: the contrast and specialization of individual character. Our study hints at an increasing attention to detail and to uniqueness of character, as familiarity develops. Vividness of elements, and their precise tuning to functional and symbolic differences, will help to provide this character. Contrast will be heightened if sharply differentiated elements are brought into close and imageable relation. Each element then takes on an intensified character of its own.

Indeed, the function of a good visual environment may not be simply to facilitate routine trips, nor to support meanings and feelings already possessed. Quite as important may be its role as a guide and a stimulus for new exploration. In a complex society, there are many interrelations to be mastered. In a democracy, we deplore isolation, extol individual development, hope for ever-widening communication between groups. If an environment has a strong visible framework and highly characteristic parts, then exploration of new sectors is both easier and more inviting. If strategic links in communication (such as museums or libraries or meeting places) are clearly set forth, then those who might otherwise neglect them may be tempted to enter.

The underlying topography, the pre-existing natural setting, is perhaps not quite as important a factor in imageability as it once used to be. The density, and particularly the extent and elaborate technology of the modern metropolis, all tend to obscure it. The contemporary urban area has man-made characteristics and problems that often override the specificity of site. Or rather, it would be more accurate to say that the specific character of a site is now perhaps as much the result of human action and desires as of the original geological structure. In addition, as the city expands, the significant "natural" factors become the larger, more fundamental ones, rather than the smaller accidents. The basic climate, the general flora and surface of a large region, the mountains and major river systems, take precedence over local features. Nevertheless, topography is still an important element in reinforcing the strength of urban elements: sharp hills can define regions, rivers and strands make strong edges, nodes can be confirmed by location at key points of terrain. The modern high-speed path is an excellent viewpoint from which to grasp topographic structure at an extensive scale.

The city is not built for one person, but for great numbers of people, of widely varying backgrounds, temperaments, occupations, and class. Our analyses indicate a substantial variation in the way different people organize their city, in what elements they most depend on, or in what form qualities are most congenial to them. The designer must therefore create a city which is as richly provided with paths, edges, landmarks, nodes, and districts as possible, a city which makes use of not just one or two form qualities, but of all of them. If so, different observers will all find perceptual material which is congenial to their own particular way of looking at the world. While one man may recognize a street by its brick pavement, another will remember its sweeping curve, and a third will have located the minor landmarks along its length.

There are, moreover, dangers in a highly specialized visible form; there is a need for a certain plasticity in the perceptual environment. If there is only one dominant path to a destination, a few sacred focal points, or an ironclad set of rigidly separated regions, then there is only one way to image the city without considerable strain. This one may suit neither the needs of all people, nor even the needs of one person as they vary from time to time. An unusual trip becomes awkward or dangerous; interpersonal relations may tend to compartment themselves; the scene becomes monotonous or restrictive.

We have taken as signs of good organization those parts of Boston in which the paths chosen by interviewees seemed to spread out rather freely. Here, presumably, the citizen is presented with a rich choice of routes to his destination, all of them well structured and identified. There is a similar value in an overlapping net of identifiable edges, so that regions big or small can be formed according to taste and need. Nodal organization gains its identity from the central focus and can fluctuate at the rim. Thus it has an advantage of flexibility over boundary organization, which breaks down if the shape of regions must change. It is important to maintain some great common forms: strong nodes, key paths, or widespread regional homogeneities. But within this large framework, there should be a certain plasticity, a richness of possible structures and clues, so that the individual observer can construct his own image: communicable, safe, and sufficient, but also supple and integrated with his own needs.

The citizen shifts his place of residence more frequently today than ever before, from area to area, from city to city. Good imageability in his environment would allow him to feel quickly at home in new surroundings. Gradual organization through long experience can less and less be relied upon. The city environment is itself changing rapidly, as techniques and functions shift. These changes are often disturbing to the citizen emotionally, and tend to disorganize his perceptual image. The techniques of design discussed in this chapter may prove useful in maintaining a visible structure and a sense of continuity even while massive changes are occurring. Certain landmarks or nodes might be retained, thematic units of district character carried over into new construction, paths salvaged or temporarily conserved.

Metropolitan Form

The increasing size of our metropolitan areas and the speed with which we traverse them raise many new problems for perception. The metropolitan region is now the functional unit of our environment, and it is desirable that this functional unit should be identified and structured by its inhabitants. The new means of communication which allow us to live and work in such a large interdependent region, could also allow us to make our images commensurate with our experiences. Such jumps to new levels of attention have occurred in the past, as jumps were made in the functional organization of life.

Total imageability of an extensive area such as a metropolitan region would not mean an equal intensity of image at every point. There would be dominant figures and more extensive backgrounds, focal points, and connective tissue. But, whether intense or neutral, each part would presumably be clear, and clearly linked to the whole. We can speculate that metropolitan images could be formed of such elements as high-speed highways, transit lines or airways; large regions with coarse edges of water or open space; major shopping nodes; basic topographic features; perhaps massive, distant landmarks.

The problem is none the less difficult, however, when it comes to composing a pattern for such an entire area. There are two techniques with which we are familiar. First, the entire region may be composed as a static hierarchy. For example, it might be organized as a major district containing three sub-districts, which each contain three sub-sub-districts, and so on. Or as another example of hierarchy, any given part of the region might focus on a minor node, these minor nodes being satellite

to a major node, while all the major nodes are arranged to culminate in a single primary node for the region.

The second technique is the use of one or two very large dominant elements, to which many smaller things may be related: the siting of settlement along a sea-coast, for example; or the design of a linear town depending on a basic communication spine. A large environment might even be radially related to a very powerful landmark, such as a central hill.

Both these techniques seem somewhat inadequate to the metropolitan problem. The hierarchical system, while congenial to some of our habits of abstract thinking, would seem to be a denial of the freedom and complexity of linkages in a metropolis. Every connection must be made in a roundabout, conceptual fashion: up to a generality and back to a particular, even though the bridging generality may have little to do with the real connection. It is the unity of a library, and libraries require the constant use of a bulky cross-referencing system.

Dependence on a strong dominant element, while giving a much more immediate sense of relation and continuity, becomes more difficult as the environment increases in size, since a dominant must be found that is big enough to be in scale with its task, and has enough "surface area" so that all the minor elements can have some reasonably close relation to it. Thus one needs a big river, for example, that winds enough to allow all settlement to be fairly near its course.

Nevertheless, these are two possible methods, and it would be useful to investigate their success in unifying large environments. Air travel may simplify the problem again, since it is (in perceptual terms) a static rather than a dynamic experience, an opportunity to see a metropolitan area almost at a glance.

Considering our present way of experiencing a large urban area, however, one is drawn toward another kind of organization: that of sequence, or temporal pattern. This is a familiar idea in music, drama, literature, or dance. Therefore it is relatively easy to conceive of, and study, the form of a sequence of events along a line, such as the succession of elements that might greet a traveler on an urban highway. With some attention, and proper tools, this experience could be made meaningful and well shaped.

It is also possible to handle the question of reversibility, i.e., the fact that most paths are traversed in both directions. The series of elements must have sequential form taken in either order, which might be accomplished by symmetry about the midpoint, or in more sophisticated ways. But the city problem continues to raise difficulties. Sequences are not only reversible, but are broken in upon at many points. A carefully constructed sequence, leading from introduction, first statement, and development to climax and conclusion, may fail utterly if a driver enters it directly at the climax point. Therefore it may be necessary to look for sequences which are interruptible as well as reversible, that is, sequences which still have sufficient imageability even when broken in upon at various points, much like a magazine serial. This might lead us from the classic start-climax-finish form to others which are more like the essentially endless, and yet continuous and variegated, patterns of jazz.

These considerations refer to organization along a single line of movement. An urban region might then be organized by a network of such organized sequences, any proposed form being tested to see if each major path, in each direction and from each entry point, was possessed of a formed sequence of elements. This is conceivable when the paths have some simple pattern such as radial convergence. It becomes more difficult to image where the network is a diffuse and intersecting one, as in a gridiron. Here the sequences work in four different directions throughout the map. Although on a much more sophisticated scale, this is akin to the problem of timing a progressive traffic-light system over a network.

It is even conceivable that one might compose in counterpoint along these lines, or from one line to another. One sequence of elements, or "melody," might be played against a countersequence. Perhaps, however, such techniques would wait upon a time when there is a more attentive and critical audience.

Even this dynamic method, the organization of a network of formed sequences, does not yet seem ideal. The environment is still not being treated as a whole but rather as a collection of parts (the sequences) arranged so as not to interfere with each other. Intuitively, one could imagine that there might be a way of creating a *whole* pattern, a pattern that would only gradually be sensed and developed by sequential experiences, reversed and interrupted as they might be. Although felt as a whole, it would not need to be a highly unified pattern with a single center or an isolating boundary. The principal quality would be sequential continuity in which each part flows from the next—a sense of interconnectedness at any level or in any direction. There would be particular zones that for any one individual might be more intensely felt or organized, but the region would be continuous, mentally traversable in any order. This possibility is a highly speculative one: no satisfactory concrete examples come to mind.

Perhaps this pattern of a whole cannot exist. In that case, the previously mentioned techniques remain as possibilities in the organization of large regions: the hierarchy, the dominant element, or the network of sequences. Hopefully, these techniques would require no more than the metropolitan planning controls now sought for other reasons, but this also remains to be seen.

The Process of Design

Any existing, functioning urban area has structure and identity, even if only in weak measure. Jersey City is a long step upward from pure chaos. If it were not, it would be uninhabitable. Almost always, a potentially powerful image is hidden in the situation itself, as in the Palisades of Jersey City, its peninsular shape, and its relation to Manhattan. A frequent problem is the sensitive reshaping of an already existing environment: discovering and preserving its strong images, solving its perceptual difficulties, and, above all, drawing out the structure and identity latent in the confusion.

At other times, the designer faces the creation of a new image, as when extensive redevelopment is underway. This problem is particularly significant in the suburban extensions of our metropolitan regions, where vast stretches of what is essentially a new landscape must be perceptually organized. The natural features are no longer a sufficient guide to structure, because of the intensity and scale of the development being applied to them. At the present tempo of building, there is no time for the slow adjustment of form to small, individualized forces. Therefore we must depend far more than formerly on conscious design: the deliberate manipulation of the world for sensuous ends. Although possessed of a rich background of former examples of urban design, the operation must now proceed at an entirely different scale of space and time.

These shapings or reshapings should be guided by what might be called a "visual plan" for the city or metropolitan region: a set of recommendations and controls which would be concerned with visual form on the urban scale. The preparation of such a plan might begin with an analysis of the existing form and public image of the area, using the techniques rising out of this study which are detailed in Appendix B. This analysis would conclude with a series of diagrams and reports illustrating the significant public images, the basic visual problems and opportunities, and the critical image elements and element interrelations, with their detailed qualities and possibilities for change.

Using this analytical background, but not limited thereby, the designer could proceed to develop a visual plan at the city scale, whose object would be to strengthen the public image. It might prescribe the location or preservation of landmarks, the development of a visual hierarchy of paths, the establishment of thematic units for districts, or the creation or clarification of nodal points. Above all, it would deal with the interrelations of elements, with their perception in motion, and with the conception of the city as a total visible form.

Substantial physical change may not be justified on this esthetic score alone, except at strategic points. But the visual plan could influence the form of physical changes which occur for other reasons. Such a plan should be fitted into all the other aspects of planning for the region, to become a normal and integral part of the comprehensive plan. Like all the other parts of this plan, it would be in a continuous state of revision and development.

The controls employed to achieve visual form at the city scale could range from general zoning provisions, advisory review, and persuasive influence over private design, to strict controls at critical points and to the positive design of public facilities such as highways or civic buildings. Such techniques are not in principle very different from controls used in the pursuit of other planning objectives. It will probably be more difficult to gain an understanding of the problem and to develop the necessary design skill than it will be to obtain the necessary powers, once the objective is clear. There is much to be done before far-reaching controls are justified.

The final objective of such a plan is not the physical shape itself but the quality of an image in the mind. Thus it will be equally useful to improve this image by training the observer, by teaching him to *look* at his city, to observe its manifold forms and how they mesh with one another. Citizens could be taken into the street, classes could be held in the schools and universities, the city could be made an animated museum of our society and its hopes. Such education might be used, not only to develop the city image, but to reorient after some disturbing change. An art of city design will wait upon an informed and critical audience. Education and physical reform are parts of a continuous process.

Heightening the observer's attention, enriching his experience, is one of the values that the mere effort to give form can offer. To some degree, the very process of reshaping a city to improve its imageability may itself sharpen the image, regardless of how unskillful the resulting physical form may be. Thus the amateur painter begins to see the world around him; the novice decorator begins to take pride in her living room and to judge others. Although such a process can become sterile if not accompanied by increasing control and judgment, even awkward "beautification" of a city may in itself be an intensifier of civic energy and cohesion.

V.

A NEW SCALE

The first chapter pointed out the special nature of city perception and concluded that the art of urban design must therefore be essentially different from the other arts. The vividness and coherence of the environmental image was singled out as being a crucial condition for the enjoyment and use of the city.

This image is the result of a two-way process between observer and observed, in which the external physical shape upon which a designer can operate plays a major role. Five elements of the urban image were distinguished, and their qualities and interrelations discussed at length. Much of the data used in this discussion came from an analysis of the form and public image of the central areas of three American cities. In the course of these analyses, methods of field reconnaissance and sample interviews for imageability were developed.

Although most of the work was confined to the identity and structure of single elements, and their patterning in small complexes, it was directed toward a future synthesis of city form considered as a whole pattern. A clear and comprehensive image of the entire metropolitan region is a fundamental requirement for the future. If it can be developed, it will raise the experience of a city to a new level, a level commensurate with the contemporary functional unit. Image organization at this scale involves wholly new design problems.

Large-scale imageable environments are rare today. Yet the spatial organization of contemporary life, the speed of movement, and the speed and scale of new construction, all make it possible and necessary to construct such environments by conscious design. This study points out, even if only in an elementary way, one approach to this new kind of design. It is the thesis of these pages that a large city environment *can* have sensuous form. To design such a form is rarely attempted today: the entire problem is either neglected or relegated to the piecemeal application of architectural or site-planning principles.

It is clear that the form of a city or of a metropolis will not exhibit some gigantic, stratified order. It will be a complicated pattern, continuous and whole, yet intricate and mobile. It must be plastic to the perceptual habits of thousands of citizens, open-ended to change of function and meaning, receptive to the formation of new imagery. It must invite its viewers to explore the world.

True enough, we need an environment which is not simply well organized, but poetic and symbolic as well. It should speak of the individuals and their complex society, of their aspirations and their historical tradition, of the natural setting, and of the complicated functions and movements of the city world. But clarity of structure and vividness of identity are first steps to the development of strong symbols. By appearing as a remarkable and well-knit *place,* the city could provide a ground for the clustering and organization of these meanings and associations. Such a sense of place in itself enhances every human activity that occurs there, and encourages the deposit of a memory trace.

By the intensity of its life and the close packing of its disparate people, the great city is a romantic place, rich in symbolic detail. It is for us both splendid and terrifying, "the landscape of our confusions," as Flanagan calls it.[21] Were it legible, truly visible, then fear and confusion might be replaced with delight in the richness and power of the scene.

In the development of the image, education in seeing will be quite as important as the reshaping of what is seen. Indeed, they together form a circular, or hopefully a spiral, process: visual education impelling the citizen to act upon his visual world, and this action causing him to see even more acutely. A highly developed art of urban design is linked to the creation of a critical and attentive audience. If art and audience grow together, then our cities will be a source of daily enjoyment to millions of their inhabitants.

Appendices

A.

SOME REFERENCES TO ORIENTATION

We can look for references to the environmental image in many places: in literature ancient and modern, in books of travel or exploration, in newspaper accounts, or in psychological and anthropological studies. Such references are generally scattered, but are frequent and revealing. While skimming through them, we will learn something about how such images are formed, what some of their characteristics are, and how they seem to play a social, psychological, and esthetic, as well as a practical, part in our lives.

From the accounts of anthropologists, for example, we infer that primitive man is normally deeply attached to the landscape he lives in; he distinguishes and names its minor parts. Observers refer to the multitude of place names, even in uninhabited country, and to the extraordinary interest in geography. The environment is an integral part of primitive cultures; the people work, create, and play in harmony with their landscape. Most often, they feel completely identified with it, are loath to leave it; it stands for continuity and stability in an uncertain world.[4, 38, 55, 62] The people of Tikopia (Santa Cruz Islands) say:

> The land stands, but man dies; he weakens and is buried down below. We dwell for but a little while, but the land stands in its abiding-place.[19]

These environments are not only highly meaningful, but their image is a vivid one.

Certain holy areas may become very highly charged, so that there is a strong focusing of attention, a fine differentiation of parts, a high density of names. The Athenian Acropolis, saturated with a long cultural and religious history, was evidently named and parceled to the gods small area by small area, almost stone by stone, making renovations extremely difficult. The Emily Gap, a small gorge 100 yards long by 30 yards wide in the MacDonnell ranges of central Australia, is to the native people a veritable gallery of legendary locations.[72] In Tikopia, the Marae, a sacred cleared space in the forest, was used ritually only once a year. It was a small rectangle, yet contained over twenty locations with regular fixed names.[19] Among more advanced cultures an entire city may be holy, such as Meshed in Iran, or Lhasa in Tibet.[16, 68] These cities are full of names and memories, distinctive forms, and holy places.

Our environmental image is still a fundamental part of our equipment for living, but for most people it is probably much less vivid and particular today. In a recent story of fantasy, C. S. Lewis imagines that he has entered someone else's mind, and is moving about in her image of the outside world.[43] There is a gray light, but nothing that could be called a sky. There are vague, dingy green shapes, blob-like, without anatomy, that he peers at and finally identifies as Shoddy Trees. There is soft stuff underneath, of a dull grassy color but without separate blades. The closer he looks, the more vague and smudged it all becomes.

The environmental image has its original function in permitting purposeful mobility. A correct map might mean life or death to a primitive tribe, as when the Luritcha of central Australia, driven from their territory by four years of drought, survive by the precise topographic memory of the oldest men.[55] These elders, from experience gained years before, and from the instructions of their grandfathers, knew the chain of tiny water holes that led them out across the desert to safety. The value of being able to distinguish stars or currents or sea-colors is obvious to the South Sea navigator, for when he sets out to strike his tiny goal he engages in a gamble with death. Knowledge of this kind allows mobility, which may make possible a better standard of living. On Puluwat (Caroline Islands), for example, there was a famous native school of navigation. Because of this skill the people of Puluwat were pirates, able to raid the islands within a wide circle.

Although such skills might seem unimportant today, we see things in a different light if we consider the cases of men who, through brain injury, have lost the ability to organize their surroundings.[15, 47, 51] They may be able to speak and think rationally, even to recognize objects without difficulty, but they cannot structure their images into any connected system. These men cannot find their own rooms again after leaving them, and must wander helplessly until conducted home, or until by chance they stumble upon some familiar detail. Purposeful movement is accomplished only by an elaborate memorization of sequences of distinctive detail, so closely spaced that the next detail is always within close range of the previous landmark. Locations normally identified by many objects in context may be recognizable only by virtue of some distinctive, separate symbol. One man recognizes a room by a small sign, another knows a street by the tram car numbers. If the symbols are tampered with, the man is lost. The whole situation parallels, in a curious fashion, the way in which we proceed in an unfamiliar city. In the case of brain injury, however, the situation is inescapable, and its practical and emotional significance is manifest.

The terror of being lost comes from the necessity that a mobile organism be oriented in its surroundings. Jaccard quotes an incident of native Africans who became disoriented.[37] They were stricken with panic, and plunged wildly into the brush. Witkin [81] tells of an experienced pilot who lost his orientation to the vertical, and who described it as the most terrifying experience of his life. Many other writers,[5, 52, 76] in describing the phenomenon of temporary disorientation in the modern city, speak of the accompanying emotions of distress. Binet mentions a man who took care to arrive at one particular railroad depot in Lyons when coming from Paris, because, although it was less convenient, it concurred with his (mistaken) image of the side of Lyons which lay toward Paris.[5] Another subject felt a slight dizziness throughout his stay in a small town, because of the persistence of a mistaken orientation. The uncomfortable tenacity of an original and incorrect organization of the environment is attested in many sources.[23] On the other hand, in the highly artificial and seemingly neutral situation of a laboratory maze, Brown reports that subjects developed affection for such simple landmarks as a rough board, which they recognized as familiar.[8]

Way-finding is the original function of the environmental image, and the basis on which its emotional associations may have been founded. But the image is valuable not only in this immediate sense in which it acts as a map for the direction of movement; in a broader sense it can serve as a general frame of reference within which the individual can act, or to which he can attach his knowledge. In this way it is like a body of belief, or a set of social customs: it is an organizer of facts and possibilities.

The differentiated landscape may simply exhibit the presence of other groups or symbolic places. Malinowski, in discussing agriculture in the Trobriand Islands off the New Guinea coast, describes the tall groves which rise above the jungle brush and clearings, and which indicate villages or tabooed tree clumps.[46] In a similar way, tall campaniles mark the locations of towns throughout the flat Venetian plain, or grain elevators the settlements of the American Midwest.

The environmental image may go further, and act as an organizer of activity. Thus, on the island of Tikopia, there were several traditional resting-places on a trail that the people used to and from their daily work.[19] Such locations gave form to the daily "commute." In the sacred Marae on this island, a small clearing packed with place-names, the minuteness of distinction of locale was an essential feature of the complexly organized rituals. In central Australia, since the legendary heroes of the natives moved along certain "dreamtime" roads, these channels are strong parts of the landscape image, and the natives feel safe in traveling them.[53] In Pratolini's autobiographical novel, he gives a striking example of people who in their daily walks continued to follow streets that no longer existed but were only imaginary tracks through a razed and empty section of Florence.[56]

At other times, distinguishing and patterning the environment may be a basis for the ordering of knowledge. Rattray speaks with great admiration of the Ashanti medicine men who strove to know every plant, animal, and insect in their forests by name, and to understand the spiritual properties of each. They were able to "read" their forests as a complex and ever-unfolding document.[61]

The landscape plays a social role as well. The named environment, familiar to all, furnishes material for common memories and symbols which bind the group together and allow them to communicate with one another. The landscape serves as a vast mnemonic system for the retention of group history and ideals. Porteus denies that the Arunta tribes of Australia have any special memory ability, although they can repeat extremely long traditional tales. Every detail of the countryside is a cue for some myth, and each scene prompts the recollection of their common culture.[55] Maurice Halbwachs makes the same point in reference to modern Paris, when he remarks that the stable physical scene, the common memory of Parisians, is a potent force in binding them together and allowing them to communicate with each other.[34]

The symbolic organization of the landscape may help to assuage fear, to establish an emotionally safe relationship between men and their total environment. A quotation regarding the Luritcha people of central Australia illustrates the point.

To each Luritcha child born in the shadow of these huge strange rocks, vast enough to awe the imagination of the white man whose eyes have beheld many wonders, the legends which identify them with the history of his own people must seem a source of great comfort. If these great rocks arose merely to mark the wanderings of his own spirit ancestors, it puts them in familiar relation with him. Legends and myths are more than tales told to while away the hours of darkness, they are part of the means by which the savage fortifies himself against the fear of the awesome and the unknown. Naturally tormented as the primitive man's mind is by the fears that are the product of loneliness, it is little wonder that he eagerly seizes on the idea that this vast, indifferent, if not inimical, Nature commemorates in many of its most striking features his tribal history, and is by the practice of magic subject to his control.[55]

Even in situations less lonely or frightening, there is a pleasant sense of familiarity or rightness in a recognized landscape. The Netsilik Eskimo put this well-worn idea in their own way: "to be surrounded by the smell of one's own things."

Indeed, the very naming and distinguishing of the environment vivifies it, and thereby adds to the depth and poetry of human experience. Passes in Tibet may have such titles as "The Vulture's Difficulty," or the "Pass of the Iron Dagger," which are not only highly descriptive but are poetic evocations of parts of Tibetan culture.[3] An anthropologist makes this comment about the Arunta landscape:

No one who has not experienced it can appreciate the vivid reality of the myths. The whole country through which we passed was apparently only mulga scrub, a few gum creeks, a low or high range here or there, or some open plains, yet it was made a scene of much activity by aboriginal history. . . . So vivid are the tales that the investigator has the feeling of an inhabited area with much activity around: people hurrying hither and thither.[54]

While today we may have more organized ways of referring to our environment — by coordinates, numbering systems, or abstract names — we often miss this quality of vivid concreteness, of unmistakable form.[40]   Wohl and Strauss give many examples of the effort of people to find a shorthand physical symbol for the city they live in, both to organize their impressions of it and in order to carry on their daily activity.[82]

The feeling and value of an imageable environment are well summed up in Proust's moving description (in "Du Coté de chez Swann") of the church steeple in Combray, where he spent many childhood summers. Not only does this piece of landscape symbolize and locate the town, but it enters deeply into every daily activity, and remains in his mind as an apparition for which he still searches in later life:

> It was always to the steeple that one must return, always it which dominated everything else, summing up the houses with an unexpected pinnacle.[57]

Types of Reference Systems

These, images may be organized in different ways.   There may be an abstract and generalized system of reference, at times explicit, at times rather a habitual manner of referring to the locations or relations of features.   The Chukchee of Siberia distinguish 22 compass directions, three-dimensional and tied to the sun.   They include the zenith and the nadir, midnight (north) and midday (south), all of which are fixed, plus 18 others which are defined by the sun positions at various times of the day or night, and therefore change with the seasons.   This system is of sufficient importance to control the orientation of all sleeping rooms.[6]   The Micronesian voyagers of the Pacific used a precise directional system, which was not, however, symmetrical but was tied to constellations and to island directions.   The number of directions varied up to 28 or 30.[18]

The system used on the North China plain is a strictly regular one. It has deep magical connotations: north being equated with black and evil, south with red, joy, life, and the sun.   It controls very strictly the placing of all religious objects and permanent structures. Indeed, the chief use of the "south-pointing needle," a Chinese invention, was not for navigation at sea, but for the orientation of buildings.   So pervasive is this system that the country people on this flat land give directions by compass points, and not by right or left, as would be natural to us.   The organizing system does not center on the individual, moving and turning with him, but is fixed, universal, and outside the person.[80]

The Arunta of Australia, in referring to an object, habitually give its proximity, orientation, and visibility with reference to the speaker. An American geographer, on the other hand, once presented a paper on the necessity for orientation to our own four cardinal points, and was surprised to find from his audience that for many city people, accustomed to orient to conspicuous urban features, this is no necessity at all. He himself was brought up in open country, in the sight of mountains.[52] For an Eskimo or an inhabitant of the Sahara, constant directions may be recognized, not by heavenly objects, but by prevailing winds, or by sand or snow formations which are the products of such winds.[37]

In parts of Africa the key direction may not be an abstract, constant one, but rather the direction toward the home territory. Thus Jaccard cites a joint encampment of several tribes, who spontaneously grouped themselves into sectors which pointed toward their own territories.[37] Later he mentions the case of French commission merchants who have business in a succession of cities strange to them. They assert that they pay little attention to names or landmarks, but simply keep a continuous mental record of the direction back to the railroad station, and strike out for it directly when their work is done. Australian grave-mounds, as another example, are shaped with reference to the direction toward the individual's totem center, or spiritual home.[72]

The island of Tikopia is an example of another sort of system, which is neither universal, egocentric, nor directed toward a base point, but is tied to a particular edge in the landscape. The island is small enough so that one is rarely out of sight or sound of the sea, and the islanders use the expressions *inland* or *seaward* for all kinds of spatial reference. An axe lying on a house-floor is localized in this way, and· Firth reports overhearing one man say to another: "There is a spot of mud on your seaward cheek." This reference pattern is so strong that they have difficulty in conceiving of any really large land mass. The villages are strung along the edge of the beach, and the traditional terms of guidance refer only to "the next village" or the one ·beyond the next, and so on. This is an easily referenced, one-dimensional series.[19]

Sometimes the environment is organized, not by a general directional system, but by one or more intensive foci, toward which other things seem to "point." In Meshed (Iran) extreme sacredness attaches to every object near the central shrine, including the dust which falls on the precinct. The high point on the approach to the city, from which the traveler first sees this mosque, is in itself important, and within the city it is proper to bow when crossing every street that leads to the shrine. This sacred focus polarizes and organizes the entire surrounding area.[16] This is comparable to the custom of genuflecting in a Roman Catholic Church when crossing the axis of the altar, which orients the church interior.

The city of Florence was organized this way in its centuries of greatness. At that time, description and locational references were made in terms of the "canti," that is, the focal points, which were such things as loggias, lights, coats of arms, tabernacles, important family houses, and key stores, especially pharmacies. Only later, the names of the canti attached themselves to the streets, which were subsequently regularized and signposted in 1785. Progressive house numbering was introduced in 1808, and the city shifted over to reference by paths.[11]

Imaging and referencing by districts was very common in older cities, where quarters and their populations were relatively stable, isolated and distinctive. In Imperial Rome, addresses were given solely by small defined districts. Presumably, arrival at such a district allowed one to proceed to one's final destination by personal inquiry.[35]

The landscape may be patterned by the lines of movement. In the case of the Arunta in Australia the entire territory is magically organized by a network of mythical paths linking together a series of isolated totemic "countries" or clan estates, and leaving waste areas between. There is normally only one correct trail to the sacred storehouse containing totemic objects, and Pink tells of the long detour made by one of his guides to approach a sacred place properly.[54]

Jaccard speaks of a famous Arab guide in the Sahara, who could follow the faintest trail, and for whom the entire desert was a network of paths. In one instance he followed painstakingly the continuous twists of the scarcely-marked way, even while his destination was clearly visible to him across the open desert. This reliance was habitual, since storms and mirages often made distant landmarks unreliable.[37] Another author writes of the Saharan *Medjbed,* the transcontinental path worn by camels that goes for hundreds of kilometers over the empty land from water hole to water hole, marked by piles of stones at crossing points. It may mean death to lose it. He speaks of the strong personality, the almost sacred character, that this trace acquires.[24] In quite another landscape, the seemingly impenetrable African forest, the tangle is intersected by elephant paths, which natives learn and traverse as we might learn and traverse city streets.[37]

Proust gives a vivid example of the sensation of a path reference system in his description of Venice:

> My gondola followed the course of the small canals; like the mysterious hand of a Genie leading me through the maze of this oriental city, they seemed, as I advanced, to be carving a road for me through the heart of a crowded quarter which they clove asunder, barely dividing with a slender fissure, arbitrarily carved, the tall houses with their tiny Moorish windows; and, as though the magic guide had been holding a candle in his hand and were lighting the way for me, they kept casting ahead of them a ray of sunlight for which they cleared a path.[58]

Brown, in his experiments in putting subjects blindfolded through a maze for the feet, found that even in this very restricted situation subjects seemed to use at least three different kinds of orientation: a memorization of the sequence of movements, usually difficult to reconstruct except in correct sequence; a set of landmarks (rough boards, sound sources, rays of sunlight that gave warmth) which identified localities; and a general sense of orientation in the room space (for example, the solution might be imaged as a general movement around the four sides of the room, with two excursions into the interior).[8]

Formation of the Image

The creation of the environmental image is a two-way process between observer and observed. What he sees is based on exterior form, but how he interprets and organizes this, and how he directs his attention, in its turn affects what he sees. The human organism is highly adaptable and flexible, and different groups may have widely different images of the same outer reality.

Sapir gives an interesting example of this differential focus of attention, in the language of the southern Paiute. They have single terms in their vocabulary for such precise topographical features as a "spot of level ground in mountains surrounded by ridges" or "canyon wall receiving sunlight" or "rolling country intersected by several small hill-ridges." Such accurate reference to topography is necessary for definite locations in a semi-arid region. He goes on to note that the characteristic Indian vocabulary does not contain the English lumping-word, "weeds," but has separate terms for these sources of food and medicine, terms which for each species distinguish whether the specimen is raw or cooked, as well as its color and stage of growth: as in the English calf, cow, bull, veal, and beef.

He mentions, on the other hand, one Indian tribe whose vocabulary does not distinguish between the sun and the moon![66]

The Aleuts have no native names for the great vertical features of their landscape: the ranges, peaks, volcanoes, and the like. Yet the tiniest horizontal aqueous feature—rill, streamlet, or pond—had its own name. Presumably this is because the tiny waterways are the environmental features which are vital for travel.[26] The attention of the Netsilik Eskimo seems also to be riveted on the aqueous features. In a group of twelve sketch maps done by natives for Rasmussen, there are 532 place names indicated by the draftsmen. Of these, 498 designate islands, coasts, bays, peninsulas, lakes, streams, or fords. Sixteen refer to hills or mountains, and only 18 make scattered reference to rocks, ravines, swamps, or settlement sites.[60] Yung makes an interesting reference to a trained geologist who was able to march unhesitatingly through foggy Alpine country, simply by his recognition of the patterning of the geologic type of the exposed rocks.[83]

Still another, and rather unusual, area of attention is sky reflection. Stefánsson says that in the Arctic low-hanging clouds of uniform color reflect the map of the earth below: those above open water being black, above sea-ice white, above soiled land-ice somewhat darker, and so on. This is of great value in crossing wide bays, where the landmarks are below the horizon.[73] These sky reflections are commonly used in the South Seas, not only to locate an island below the horizon but even to identify it by the color and shape of the reflection. Some idea of the great range of forms which are available for orientation may be gained by a reading of Gatty's latest book on navigation.[23]

These cultural differences may extend not only to the features receiving attention but also to the way in which they are organized. The Aleutian Islands have no generic name in the native tongue, since the Aleuts do not recognize what to us appears to be the obvious unity of the chain.[17] The Arunta group the stars quite differently than we do, frequently putting bright, close stars in different groups, while linking faint and distant ones.[45]

So adaptable is our perceptual mechanism, moreover, that every human group can distinguish the parts of its landscape, can perceive and give meaning to significant detail. This occurs no matter how undifferentiated that world may seem to an outside observer, This is true of the endless grey mulga thicket which is part of the Australian landscape; the flat snow-covered land of the Eskimo, where even the distinction between land and sea is lost; the foggy, shifting Aleutians; or the open "trackless" ocean of the Polynesian navigator.

Two primitive groups developed a science of direction-finding and geography which was only recently surpassed by western mapmaking. These are the Eskimo and the navigators of the South Seas. The Eskimo are able to construct usable maps, freehand, covering territories sometimes 400 or 500 miles in one dimension. This is a feat of which few people anywhere are capable, without prior reference to constructed maps.

Similarly, the trained navigators of the Caroline Islands in the Pacific had an elaborate system of sailing directions which were carefully related to constellations, island locations, winds, currents, sun positions, and wave directions.[18, 44] Arago stated that a celebrated pilot once represented all the islands in the archipelago for him by grains of maize, marked their relative position, named each one, and stated the accessibility and products of each. This archipelago is some 1500 miles from east to west! Furthermore, he made a compass from bamboo, and indicated the prevailing winds, constellations, and currents by which he guided himself.

Both cultures producing these triumphs of abstract ability and perceptual attention had two things in common: first, their environments of snow or water were essentially featureless or differentiated only subtly, and second, both groups were forced to be mobile. The Eskimo must travel seasonally from one type of hunting to another, if he is to survive. The best seafarers in the South Seas did not come from the fertile high islands but from the tiny low islands, where natural resources were scanty and famine was always close. The nomad Touareg, in the empty Sahara, are a similar group, and have an almost equal ability. On the other hand, Jaccard notes that native Africans, of sedentary agricultural habit, easily become lost in their own forests.[37]

The Role of Form

Nevertheless, having said so much about the flexibility and adaptability of human perception, we must now add that the shape of the physical world plays its part, as well. The very fact that skilled navigation arose in what would seem to be perceptually difficult environments indicates the influence of these outward shapes.

The ability to distinguish and orient in these resistant environments is not achieved without cost. The knowledge was usually limited to specialists. Rasmussen's informants who drew his maps were chiefs—many other Eskimos could not do it. Cornetz remarks that there were only a dozen good guides in all south Tunisia.[13] The navigators in Polynesia were the ruling caste. Knowledge was transmitted from father to son, and there was, as mentioned above, a formal school in the subject on the island of Puluwat. It was customary for the navigators to eat at a separate mess, where the talk was constantly of directions and currents. This is reminiscent of Mark Twain's Mississippi River pilots, who were constantly discussing and riding up and down the river, and thus keeping abreast of its treacherous shifting landmarks.[77] Admirable as this skill is, it is some distance from an easy and familiar relation with the environment. Polynesian sea voyages were evidently accompanied by real anxiety, a usual sailing formation being a long row of canoes abreast to aid in finding land. Among the Arunta of Australia, as another example, it is only the old men who can lead from water-hole to water-hole or who can correctly locate the proper sacred path in the mulga thicket. On the well-differentiated island of Tikopia, the problem could hardly come up.

We have frequent accounts of native guides who lose orientation in featureless surroundings. Strehlow describes floundering for hours in the Australian mulga thicket with an experienced native, who repeatedly climbed trees in the effort to get his bearings from distant landmarks.[75] Jaccard recites the tragic cases of lost Touareg.[37]

At the other end of the scale, there are visual qualities in some landscape features which make them the inevitable subjects of attention, despite the selective power of the eye. Most often, sacredness is concentrated in the more striking natural features, such as the connection of the Ashanti gods with the great lakes and rivers, or the common reverence attached to great mountains. So in Assam there is a famous hill which is the legendary site of Buddha's death. It is described as bold and picturesque by Waddell, rising directly from a plain to which it is in sharp contrast. He then notes that it was worshipped by the aborigines long before, and has become holy for Brahmans and Mohammedans as well.[78]

For physical reasons, the great mountain on Tikopia Island is the central organizing feature. It is the crowning point of the island, both sociologically and topographically, the place of descent of the gods. It marks the location of home from far out to sea, and has an aura of the supernatural. Since the crest is rarely cleared and planted to taro, there is a peculiar flora here which is lacking down below, and this reinforces the special interest of the place.[19]

Occasionally, a landscape may be so fantastically differentiated as to compel attention. Kawaguchi describes the banks of a river near Lake Kholgyal in Tibet:

> . . . rocks piled up here and there, some yellow, some crimson, others blue, still others green, and some others purple . . . the rocks were highly fantastic, some sharp and angular, others protruded over the river. The nearer bank . . . was full of queerly shaped rocks, and each of those rocks bore a name . . . all these were objects of veneration to the common people.[39]

To take a humbler example, the territories defended by nesting birds in a meadow have been mapped over a succession of years. These territories show wide fluctuations and reorganizations, as might be expected from their occupation by different individuals. But certain perceptually strong boundaries of fence or brush remain stable throughout the shifts.[50] Migrating birds, advancing in a general direction over a broad front, are known to direct their flight and follow along major "leading lines," or edges formed by topographic features such as seacoasts. Even swarms of locusts, who maintain cohesion and direction with reference to the wind, become disorganized and scattered when they move out over featureless water surfaces.

Other features may not only be noticeable and distinguishable but even have a "presence," a sort of animation or peculiarly vivid reality, that is felt by peoples of utterly different cultures. Kawaguchi speaks of a holy mountain in Tibet, seen for the first time as "sitting with an air of great solemnity," and likens it to his own Buddha Vairochana, flanked by Bodhisattvas.[39]

A similar experience, closer to home, was the original impact of a particular escarpment along the Oregon Trail:

> . . . as the west-bound party drew abreast of the bluffs a wave of astonishment swept through it. . . . Numerous observers discovered lighthouses, brick kilns, the capitol at Washington, Beacon Hill, shot towers, churches, spires, cupolas, streets, workshops, stores, warehouses, parks, squares, pyramids, castles, forts, pillars, domes, minarets, temples, Gothic castles, 'modern' fortifications, French cathedrals, Rhineland castles, towers, tunnels, hallways, mausoleums, a Temple of Belus, and hanging gardens. . . . Taken at a glance the rocks 'had the appearance of Cities, Temples, Castles, Towers, Palaces, and every variety of great and magnificent structures . . . splendid edifices, like beautiful white marble, fashioned in the style of every age and country. . .[69]

Many observers are quoted, to indicate the common and overwhelming impact of these special geological shapes.

Therefore, while noting the flexibility of human perception, it must be added that outer physical shape has an equally important role. There are environments which invite or reject attention, which facilitate or resist organization or differentiation. This is analogous to the ease or difficulty with which the adaptable human brain can memorize associated or unassociated material.

Jaccard mentions several "classical locations" in Switzerland where people are consistently unable to maintain direction.[36] Peterson notes that the organization of his image of Minneapolis typically breaks down each time the street gridiron changes its orientation.[52] Trowbridge finds that most people are unable to point to distant cities from New York without gross errors, but that Albany is an exception, since it is visibly linked by the Hudson River.[76]

In London, a small development called Seven Dials was built about 1695, consisting of seven streets which converged on a circular junction containing a Doric pillar bearing seven sun dials, each facing one of the radiating streets. Gay refers to the confusing shape of this area in his *Trivia*, although he implies that it is only the peasant, the stupid outsider, who could be befuddled by it.[25]

Malinowski draws a sharp distinction between the differentiated volcanic landscape of Dobu and the Amphletts in the D'Entrecasteaux Islands near New Guinea, versus the monotonous coral islands of the Trobriands. These island groups are connected by regular trading expeditions, and the concentration of mythical meaning in the Dobu area, as well as the reactions of the Trobrianders to this imageable volcanic landscape, is described in his pages. Speaking of the trip from the Trobriands to Dobu, Malinowski says:

> The low strip of land, which surrounds the Trobriand lagoon in a wide sweep, thins away and dissolves in the haze, and before them the southern mountains rise higher and higher. . . . The nearest of them, Koyatabu, a slim, somewhat tilted pyramid, forms a most alluring beacon, guiding the mariners due south. . . . Within a day or two these disembodied misty forms are to assume what for the Trobrianders seems marvellous shape and enormous bulk. They are to surround the Kula traders with their solid walls of precipitous rock and green jungle. . . . The Trobrianders will sail deep, shaded bays . . . beneath the transparent waters a marvellous world of multi-colored coral, fish and seaweed will unfold itself . . . they will also find wonderful heavy, compact stones of various shapes and colors, whereas at

home the only stone is the insipid, white dead coral . . . besides many types of granite and basalt and volcanic tuff, specimens of black obsidian, with its sharp edge and metallic ring, and sites full of red and yellow ochre. . . . Thus the landscape now before them is a sort of promised land, a country spoken of in almost legendary tone.[46]

In a similar way, although the "dream-time" roads of Australia pass in every direction over a land which is largely level mulga plain, yet the legendary camp sites, the nodes of sacred history and attention, seem to be heavily concentrated in the two regions of differentiated landscape: the MacDonnell and the Stuart's Bluff Ranges.

Parallel to these comparisons of primitive landscapes we may put Eric Gill's comparison of Brighton, England where he was born, to Chichester, to which he moved in his adolescence:

> It had simply never occurred to me before that day that towns could have a shape and be, like my beloved locomotives, things with character and meaning . . . [Chichester] was a town, a city, a thing planned and ordered—no mere congeries of more or less sordid streets, growing, like a fungus, wherever the network of railways and sidings and railway sheds would allow. . . . I only knew that Chichester was what Brighton was not: an end, a thing, a place. . . . The plan of Chichester is clear and clean. . . . Over the Roman wall you could look straight out into the green fields. . . . Four straight wide main streets dividing the city into nearly equal quarters and the residential quarter similarly divided by four small streets and these almost completely filled with seventeenth- and eighteenth-century houses. . . . But Brighton, as we knew it . . . well, there is simply nothing to be said about it. When we thought of Brighton, it was of a place of which the center was our home . . . there was no other. But when we lived in Chichester . . . the center was not No. 2 North Walls, but the Market Cross. We gained not only a civic sense but a sense of ordered relations generally. . . . Brighton wasn't a place at all. It had never occurred to me that any other sort of town could exist.[33]

The perceptual clarity of the island of Tikopia, due to the presence of ·Mt. Reani, has already been mentioned. How a differentiated shape can be used in detail, is illustrated by this quotation:

> When a Tikopia sets out from his native land his first estimates of distance he has travelled are based on the portions of the island still showing above the horizon. There are five principal points on the scale. The first is the rauraro, the lowland near the shore. When this disappears, the voyager knows he is some distance out. When the

cliffs (mato) arising 200 to 300 feet in various spots round the coast become lost, another point is reached; then the uru mauna, the crests of the chain of hills ringing the lake, perhaps 500 to 800 feet in height, sink below the waves. When the uru asia (the last break in the contour of Mt. Reani, about 1000 feet) goes down, then the voyager realizes he is far out to sea; and when at last he sees the uru ronorono, the tip of the mountain itself, vanish from sight, he greets the moment with sorrow.[19]

With the aid of a favorably differentiated landscape profile, this familiar phenomenon of parting has been regularized into accepted intervals, each with both practical and emotional meaning.

When a character in a novel by Forster returns from India, he senses with sudden shock, on entering the Mediterranean, the sheer form-quality of his surroundings, their imageability:

> The buildings of Venice, like the mountains of Crete and the fields of Egypt, stood in the right place whereas in poor India everything was placed wrong. He had forgotten the beauty of form among idol temples and lumpy hills; indeed, without form, how can there be beauty? . . . In the old undergraduate days he had wrapped himself up in the many-colored blanket of St. Mark's, but something more precious than mosaics and marbles was offered to him now: the harmony between the works of man and the earth that upholds them, the civilization that has escaped muddle, the spirit in a reasonable form, with flesh and blood subsisting. Writing picture post-cards to his Indian friends, he felt that all of them would miss the joys he experienced now, the joys of form, and that this constituted a serious barrier. They would see the sumptuousness of Venice, not its shape.[22]

Disadvantages of Imageability

A highly visible environment may have its disadvantages, as well. A landscape loaded with magical meanings may inhibit practical activities. The Arunta face death rather than move to a more favorable area. The ancestral grave-mounds in China occupy desperately needed arable land, and among the Maori some of the best landing-places are forbidden because of their mythical import. Exploitation is more easily accomplished where there is no sentiment about the land. Even conservative use of resources may be impaired where habitual orientation does not allow easy adaptation to new techniques and needs.

Geoghegan refers to the richness of place names in Aleut but follows this with the interesting comment that there are so many particular names for each tiny feature that very often the Aleuts of one island have scarcely heard of the place names on another.[26] A highly differentiated system, lacking abstractness and generality, may actually reduce communication.

It may have consequences of another sort. Strehlow says of the Arunta:

> Since every feature of the landscape, prominent or otherwise, is already associated with one or the other of these myths, we can understand the utter apathy of literary efforts . . . their forefathers have left them not a single unoccupied scene which they could fill with creatures of their own imagination . . . tradition has effectually stifled creative impulse . . . native myths ceased to be invented many centuries ago . . . they are on the whole uninspired preservers . . . not so much a primitive as a decadent race.[75]

If it is desirable that an environment evoke rich, vivid images, it is also desirable that these images be communicable and adaptable to changing practical needs, and that there can develop new groupings, new meanings, new poetry. The objective might be an imageable environment which is at the same time open-ended.

As a peculiar example of how this dilemma can be resolved, even in an irrational way, we may take the Chinese pseudo science of geomantics.[32] This is a complicated lore of landscape influence, systematized and interpreted by professors. It deals with winds of evil that can be controlled by hills, rocks, or trees that visually seem to block dangerous gaps, and with good water spirits that are to be attracted by ponds, courses, and drains. The shapes of surrounding features are interpreted as symbolizing various spirits contained therein. This spirit may be accounted useful, or it may be inactive and useless. It can be concentrated or dispersed, deep or at the surface, pure or mixed, weak or strong, and must be used, controlled, or enhanced by planting, siting, towers, stones, and so forth. Possible interpretations are many and complex; it is an endlessly expanding field which experts are exploring in every direction. Divorced from reality as this pseudo science may be, yet it has for our purposes two interesting features: first, that it is an open-ended analysis of the environment: new meanings, new poetry, further developments are always possible; second, it leads to the use and control of outside forms and their influences: it emphasizes that man's foresight and energy rule the universe and can change it. Perhaps there are hints here as to ways of constructing an imageable environment that is not at the same time stifling and oppressive.

B.

THE USE OF THE METHOD

In applying the basic concept of imageability to the American city, we have used two principal methods: the interview of a small sample of citizens with regard to their image of the environment, and a systematic examination of the environmental image evoked in trained observers in the field. The value of these techniques is an important question, particularly since one of the objectives of our study was the development of adequate methods. Two different questions are contained within this general one: (a) how reliable are the methods, how truthful are they when they indicate a certain conclusion? and (b) how useful are they? Are the conclusions valuable in making planning decisions, and is the effort expended worth the result?

The basic office interview consisted in its essentials of a request for a sketch map of the city, for the detailed description of a number of trips through the city, and for a listing and brief description of the parts felt to be most distinctive or vivid in the subject's mind. This interview was conducted first in order to test the hypothesis of imageability; second, to gain some rough approximation to the public images of the three cities concerned, which might be compared to the findings of the field reconnaissance and so help to develop some suggestions for urban design; and third, to develop a short-cut method for eliciting the public image in any given city. In these objectives, the method proved reasonably successful, except that there are doubts as to the generality of the public image so gained, as will be discussed below.

The office interview itself covered the following questions:

1. What first comes to your mind, what symbolizes the word "Boston" for you? How would you broadly describe Boston in a physical sense?

2. We would like you to make a quick map of central Boston, inward or downtown from Massachusetts Avenue. Make it just as if you were making a rapid description of the city to a stranger, covering all the main features. We don't expect an accurate drawing—just a rough sketch. [Interviewer is to take notes on the sequence in which the map is drawn.]

3a. Please give me complete and explicit directions for the trip that you normally take going from home to where you work. Picture yourself actually making the trip, and describe the sequence of things you would see, hear, or smell along the way, including the pathmarkers that have become important to you, and the clues that a stranger would need to make the same decisions that you have to make. We are interested in the physical pictures of things. It's not important if you can't remember the names of streets and places. [During recital of trip, interviewer is to probe, where needed, for more detailed descriptions.]

b. Do you have any particular emotional feelings about various parts of your trip? How long would it take you? Are there parts of the trip where you feel uncertain of your location?
[Question 3 is then to be repeated for one or more trips which are standardized for all interviewees, i.e., "go on foot from Massachusetts General Hospital to South Station," or "go by car from Faneuil Hall to Symphony Hall."]

4. Now, we would like to know what elements of central Boston you think are most distinctive. They may be large or small, but tell us those that for you are the easiest to identify and remember.
[For each of two or three of the elements listed in response to 4, the interviewer goes on to ask question 5:]

5a. Would you describe _____ to me? If you were taken there blindfolded, when the blindfold was taken off what clues would you use to positively identify where you were?

b. Are there any particular emotional feelings that you have with regard to _____?

c. Would you show me on your map where _____ is? (and, if appropriate:) Where are the boundaries of it?

6. Would you show me on your map the direction of north?

7. The interview is over now, but it would help if we could just have a few minutes of free discussion. (Remainder of questions are inserted informally:)
a. What do you think we were trying to find out?
b. What importance is orientation and the recognition of city elements to people?
c. Do you feel any pleasure from knowing where you are or where you are going? Or displeasure in the reverse?
d. Do you find Boston an easy city to find your way in, or to identify its parts?
e. What cities of your acquaintance have good orientation? Why?

This was a lengthy interview, normally lasting about 1½ hours, but almost always attended with great interest by the subjects, and often with some emotion. The entire proceedings were recorded on tape and then transcribed, a clumsy procedure which nevertheless recorded full details, as well as revealing pauses and inflections of voice.

Sixteen of the Boston interviewees were sufficiently interested to arrange for a second session. Here they were first confronted with a stack of photographs of the Boston area, taken to cover the entire district in a systematic way, but given to the subject in random order. Several photographs of other cities were inserted in the collection. First the subjects were asked to classify the photographs, in whatever groups seemed natural to them, and then they were requested to identify as many of the pictures as they could, telling what clues they used to make the identification. The photographs recognized were then reassembled, and the subject was asked to lay them out on a large table as if he were placing them in their proper position on a large map of the city.

Finally, these same volunteers were taken out in the field to go through one of the earlier imaginary trips: that from Massachusetts General Hospital to South Station. They were accompanied by the interviewer, and a portable tape recorder was used. The subject was asked to lead the way, to discuss why a particular route was chosen, to point out what he saw along the way, and to indicate where he felt either confident or lost.

As an outside check on this small sample, a study was made of the answers to requests for directions made of people on the sidewalks of the city. Six standard destinations were chosen: Commonwealth Avenue, the corner of Summer and Washington Streets, Scollay Square, the John Hancock Building, Louisburg Square, and the Public Garden. Five standard origin points were likewise chosen: the main entrance of the Massachusetts General Hospital, the Old North Church in the North End, the corner of Columbus Avenue and Warren Street, the South Station, and Arlington Square. At each origin point, the sidewalk interviewer asked directions to each destination, by accosting four or five randomly chosen passers-by. He asked three questions: "How do I get to ————?"; "How will I recognize it when I get there?"; and "How long will it take me to walk there?"

To compare with these subjective pictures of the city, such data as air photos, maps, and diagrams of density, use, or building shape might seem to be the proper "objective" description of the physical form of the city. Consideration of their objectivity aside, such things are quite inadequate for the purpose, being both too superficial and yet not generalized enough. The variety of factors which might be evaluated is infinite, and it was found that the best comparison to the interviews was the record of another subjective response, but in this case a systematic and observant one, using categories which had proved significant in the analysis of earlier pilot interviews. While it was clear that the interviewees were responding to a common physical reality, the best way to define that reality was not through any quantitative, "factual" method but through the perception and evaluation of a few field observers, trained to look carefully, and with a prior set toward the kinds of urban elements that had so far seemed to be significant.

The field analysis was eventually simplified to a systematic coverage of the area on foot by a trained observer, previously instructed in the concept of city imageability. He mapped the area, indicating the presence, visibility, and the interrelations among the landmarks, nodes, paths, edges, and districts, and noting the image strength and weakness of these elements. This coverage was followed by several long "problem" trips across the area, testing the grasp of the whole structure. The observer divided the elements into categories of major or minor significance, "major" elements being those exceptionally strong or vivid, and continually asked himself why this element had strong or weak identity, why this connection seemed clear or obscure.

What is being mapped here is an abstraction, not physical reality itself but the generalized impressions that real form makes on an observer indoctrinated in a certain way. This mapping was, of course, done independently from the interview analysis, and required perhaps 3 to 4 man-days for an area of this size. The description of two elements in Appendix C will illustrate the kind of detail used in making such judgments.

In the first field analyses were developed the principal hypotheses as to types of elements, how they are put together, and what makes for strong identity. These were the hypotheses tested and refined in the interviews. A secondary objective was to develop a technique for a visual analysis of a city, which could predict the probable public image of that city. In both objectives, the method as finally devised proved successful, with the reservation that it was still too much concerned with single elements, and underemphasized their patterning into a complex visual whole.

Figures 35 to 46, pages 146 to 151

Figures 35 through 46 illustrate the images of the three cities as derived from the consensus of verbal interviews and sketch maps, and from our own field reconnaissance. For comparison, each set of city maps uses the same scale, and all use the same symbols.

A few generalizations may be made here regarding the relations between the data independently derived from interview and field reconnaissance. The field analyses in Boston and Los Angeles proved to be surprisingly accurate predictions of the images derived from the verbal interview material. In poorly differen-

Figure 47, page 152

tiated Jersey City, the field analysis predicted somewhat short of two-thirds of the interview image, but even here there are very few major elements in either source which do not appear in the other. In all cases, the relative ranking of elements is highly consistent. The field analysis, done on foot, developed two faults: a tendency to neglect minor elements important for automobile circulation, and a tendency to pass over certain minor features of districts that are especially important to subjects because of the social status they reflect. Our field method therefore, if supplemented by automobile surveys, seems to be a technique that can predict the probable composite image with some success, allowing for the "invisible" effects of social prestige, and for the more random fixing of attention in a visually undifferentiated environment.

While the correlation between an individual sketch map and the same person's interview was in some cases rather low, there was a good correlation between the composite of sketch maps, and the composite of verbal interviews. Again, major elements rarely appear in only one source. The sketch maps, however, tend to have a higher "threshold," that is, elements which appear with the lowest frequencies in the interviews tend not to appear at all in the sketches, and generally all elements are drawn less frequently than

144

they are mentioned verbally. This effect is strongest again, in Jersey City. In addition, the sketches tend to emphasize paths somewhat, and to exclude parts which are especially difficult to draw or locate, even though indentifiable, such as a "bottomless" landmark, or a very complicated street pattern. But these defects are minor and can be adjusted for. The composite sketch map, in regard to the identification of elements, bears a strong resemblance to the verbal interview.

A major discrepancy appears between the two sources, however, in regard to connections and general organization. The most important known connections persist in the sketches, but many others may disappear. Perhaps the difficulties of drawing and of fitting everything together simultaneously make the sketch maps unduly fragmented and distorted. They are not a good index of the known connective structure.

The listing of distinctive features, finally, proved to have the highest threshold of all the measures, excluding many elements which appeared on the sketches and singling out only the strongest mentions of the field analysis or the verbal interviews. This particular method seems to convey the highlights of a city—its visual essence.

The test on photographic recognition confirmed the verbal results quite well. For example, Commonwealth Avenue and the Charles River were easily recognized by over 90% of the subjects: Tremont Street, the Common, Beacon Hill, and Cambridge Street were also quickly and specifically identified. The other photographs go to confirm the pattern, down to the concentration of unrecognizability in the South End, the base of the John Hancock Building, the West End-North Station area, and the side streets of the North End.

Legend for Figures 35 to 46 following

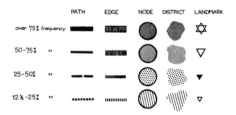

145

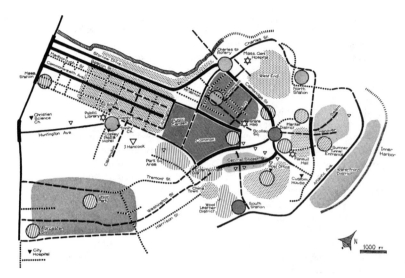

FIG. 35. *The Boston image as derived from verbal interviews*

FIG. 36. *The Boston image as derived from sketch maps*

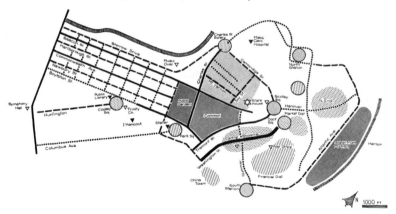

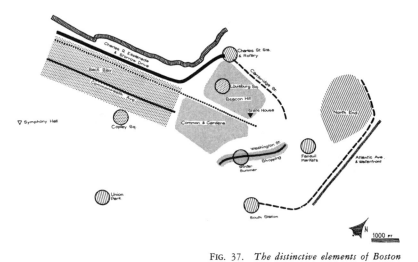

FIG. 37. *The distinctive elements of Boston*

FIG. 38. *The visual form of Boston as seen in the field*

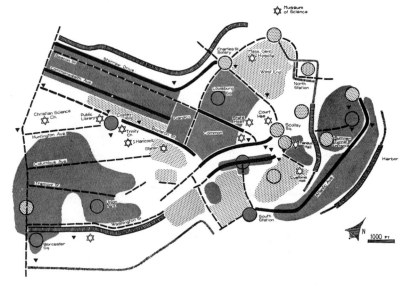

147

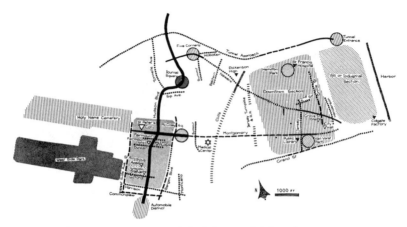

FIG. 39. *The Jersey City image as derived from verbal interviews*

FIG. 40. *The Jersey City image as derived from sketch maps*

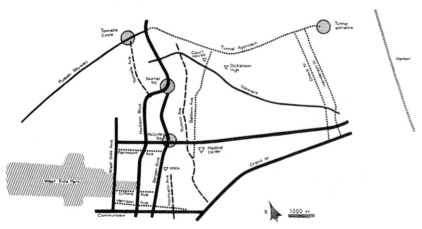

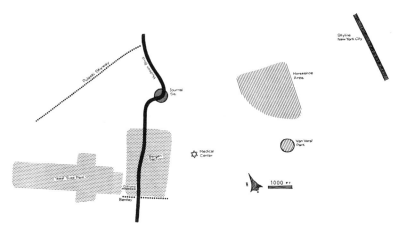

FIG. 41. *The distinctive elements of Jersey City*

FIG. 42. *The visual form of Jersey City as seen in the field*

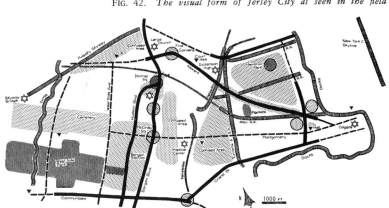

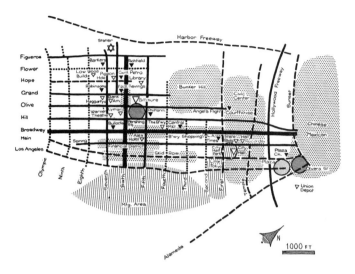

FIG. 43. *The Los Angeles image as derived from verbal interviews*

FIG. 44. *The Los Angeles image as derived from sketch maps*

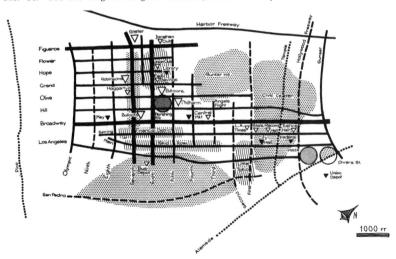

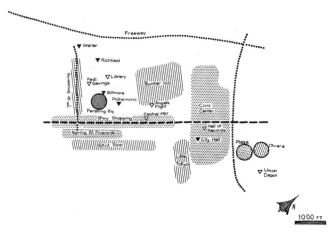

FIG. 45.   *The distinctive elements of Los Angeles*

FIG. 46.   *The visual form of Los Angeles as seen in the field*

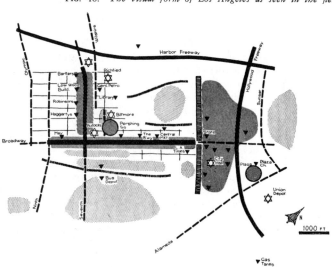

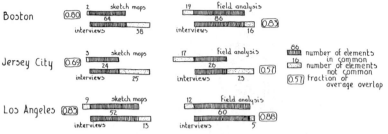

FIG. 47. *Overlap between interviews, sketch maps, and field analysis*

Figure 48

Figure 48 is a graphic compilation of elements mentioned by 160 passers-by, when stopped in the streets and questioned as noted above. Again, the composite image from these hurried interviews was strikingly similar to the other composite data. Principal differences were the greater prominence given to paths leading away from points where the questions were asked. It must be remembered that the area called into play was only that containing the set of possible paths between origins and destinations (roughly, the dashed line). The presence of blanks *outside* this area is meaningless.

While these methods revealed much internal consistency, two principal criticisms may be launched against the adequacy of the sample interviewed. First, the samples were inordinately small: thirty people in the case of Boston, and half that number in Jersey City and Los Angeles. It would be impossible to generalize from these, and to say that a "true" public image of the particular city has been uncovered. The small size was made necessary by the broad type of inquiry that was made, and by the lengthy time required for the elephantine and experimental technique of analysis. Clearly, a retest with a larger sample is needed, and this requires more rapid and precise methods.

A second criticism is the unbalanced nature of the samples chosen. They were well balanced as to age (above adolescence) and sex. All were familiar with the environment, and specialists such as city planners, engineers, and architects were excluded. But because articulate volunteers were needed for these early efforts, the sample was quite unbalanced as to class and occupation, being primarily middle-class, professional and managerial. There is bound to be a strong class bias in the results, therefore, and retests should be made with a sample that is not only larger but also more representative of the general population.

The lack of a truly random distribution of residence and work place of subjects was also unfortunate, although an effort was made to keep this bias to a minimum. The Boston sample was low in subjects coming from the North and West Ends, for example, a correlate of the class bias. The bunching is inevitable and true to life as regards work place, but should be corrected in regard to residence. Present evidence does not seem to indicate that a completely random residential distribution of subjects would change the general image as much as class balance might. Areas are often imaged strongly or weakly despite relative familiarity or unfamiliarity. The street interviews, which dealt with a much larger sample and are more nearly random in class distribution, tended in general to confirm the longer interviews, within the limits of their rather hurried information. The critique of the sample used may, therefore, be summed up in this way:

First, the internal consistency of the data received from several sources suggests that the methods used do indeed give a fairly reliable insight into the composite city image of the particular people interviewed, and that these methods are applicable to different cities. The fact that the images of different cities were different fits the hypothesis that visual form plays a significant role. Second,

FIG. 48. *The Boston image derived from the street interviews*

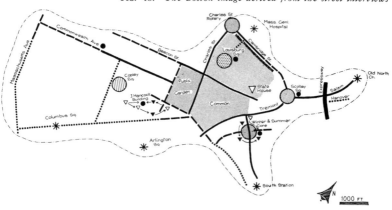

153

despite the small size, the class bias, and the partial locational bias of these samples, there was some indication that the composite image might still be a rough first approximation of the true public image. The sample size and bias must be improved in a retest, however.

Since the sample was small, no attempt was made to subdivide it further and to investigate the separate images held by different age, sex, or other groups. The sample was analyzed as a whole, and the background of subjects never taken into account except to note the general bias of the whole. Probing into group differences would undoubtedly be an interesting inquiry.

So far, of course, the study has definitely shown only the existence of a consistent image which is used to describe or recollect the city in the absence of the real thing. This might be quite different from the. image used when actually operating in the environment. The only checks on this possible discrepancy were the field trips made by some subjects, and the street interviews. The latter seemed to confirm the recollected image, although they were limited in scope and still verbal in nature. The field trip data gave an ambiguous answer. Different routes were often taken in the field as against the office interview, but the general structure seemed to be similar. Many more detailed landmarks appeared in the field recordings. Unfortunately, these recordings were for technical reasons thin and unsatisfactory. Very likely, there is a difference between the image conveyed to another person in retrospect and the image used on the spot when interperson communication is unnecessary. Yet it is also likely that these are not sharply separate, but grade one into the other. At the very least, the material shows correlations between actions and the communicated image, and indicates the strong emotional significance of the latter.

The hypothetical element types (node, district, landmark, edge, path) were in large measure confirmed by the data, after some modification. Not that such categories were proved to exist, like Platonic archetypes, but the categories were consistently able to embrace the data in a useful way, without strain. Paths proved to be the dominant element in terms of quantity, and there was a remarkable stability between the three cities in the percentage of total elements devoted to each category. The single exception was the shift in attention from paths and edges to landmarks, which was noted in Los Angeles. This was a striking change for an automobile-oriented city, but it may perhaps have been due to the lack of differentiation in the gridiron streets.

While data on single elements and element types was perhaps adequate, there was a lack of information on element interrelations, patterns, sequences, and wholes. Better methods must be evolved to approach these vital aspects.

The Method as the Basis for Design

Perhaps the best way of summarizing this general critique of method is to recommend a technique of image analysis designed to by-pass many of the difficulties cited above and developed as the basis of a plan for the future visual form of any given city.

The procedure might begin with two studies. The first would be a generalized field reconnaissance by two or three trained observers, systematically covering the city both on foot and by vehicle, by night and day, and supplementing this coverage by several "problem" trips, as described above. This would culminate in a field analysis map and brief report, which would deal with strengths and weaknesses, and with general pattern as well as parts.

A parallel step would be the mass interview of a large sample, balanced to match the general population characteristics. This group, which could be interviewed simultaneously or in several parts, would be asked to do four things:

a. Draw a quick sketch map of the area in question, showing the most interesting and important features, and giving a stranger enough knowledge to move about without too much difficulty.

b. Make a similar sketch of the route and events along one or two imaginary trips, trips chosen to expose the length and breadth of the area.

c. Make a written list of the parts of the city felt to be most distinctive, the examiner explaining the meaning of "parts" and "distinctive."

d. Put down brief written answers to a few questions of the type: "Where is _____ located?"

The tests would be analyzed for frequency of mention of elements and their connections, for sequence of drawing, and for vivid elements, sense of structure, and composite image.

The field reconnaissance and the mass interview would then be compared for the relation of public image to visual form, to make a first-round analysis of the visual strengths and weakness of the whole area, and to identify the critical points, sequences, or patterns which are worth further attention.

Second-round investigation of these critical problems would then begin. Using a small sample, subjects would be asked in individual interviews to locate selected critical elements, to operate with them in brief imaginary trips, to describe them, to make sketches of them, to discuss their feelings and memories about them. A few subjects might be taken out to these special locations, making brief field trips involving them, and describing and discussing them on the spot. Direction inquiries to the element from various origins might also be made of a random sample of persons in the street.

When these second-round studies had been analyzed for content and problems, equally intensive field reconnaissance of these same elements would then be carried out. Detailed studies of identity and structure under many different field conditions of light, distance, activity, and movement would follow. These studies would use the interview results, but would be by no means limited to them. The detailed studies of Boston elements in Appendix C are possible models.

All this material would finally be synthesized in a series of maps and reports which would give the basic public image of the area, the general visual problems and strengths, the critical elements and element interrelations, with their detailed qualities and possibilities for change. On such an analysis, continuously modified and kept up to date, a plan for the future visual form of the region could be based.

Directions for Future Research

The preceding critique, and many of the pages in earlier chapters, point to unsolved problems. Some next steps of analysis are quite obvious; others, even more important, are harder to grasp.

An obvious next step is to use the analytical technique described just above for testing a more adequate sample of the population. Conclusions from this work would be on much sounder ground, and a technique suitable for practical application could be perfected.

Our knowledge of the subject would also be enriched if comparative studies were applied to a greater range of environments than the three cities actually studied. Very new and very old cities, compact and sprawling ones, dense and sparse, chaotic and highly ordered environments, might all produce characteristic differences in their image. How does the public image of a village differ from that of Manhattan? Is a lake city easier to conceptualize than a railroad town? Such studies would produce a storehouse of material on the effects of physical form, on which the designer of cities could draw.

It would be equally interesting to apply these methods to environments of different scale or function than cities: a building, for example, or a landscape; a transportation system, or a valley region. Most important in terms of practical need is the application and adjustment of these ideas to the metropolitan region, which at present seems hopelessly beyond our perceptual grasp.

The key differences may equally likely be in the observer himself. As planning becomes a world-wide discipline, and planners are drawn into the business of making plans for people of other countries, it becomes necessary to make sure that what has been found in America is not simply a derivation of local culture. How does an Indian look at his city, or an Italian?

These differences make difficulties for the analyst, not only in international practice but within his own country as well. He can be prisoner of a regional way of thought or, particularly in America, of that of his own class. If cities are to be used by many groups of people, then it is important to understand how the different major groups tend to image their surroundings. The same might be said of significant variations in personality type. The present study dealt only in the common factors within the sample.

It would be of interest to see whether some of the image types that seemed to appear—those using static hierarchical systems versus those using dynamic unrolling connections; or those using concrete versus abstract images, for example—are stable, non-transferable types, or are simply the result of a particular training or milieu. How, furthermore, do some of these types interrelate? Can a dynamic image system also be one that is positionally structured? The relation between the communicable memory image and the image used in immediate field operations might also be investigated.

All these questions have more than theoretical interest. Cities are the habitat of many groups, and only with a differentiated understanding of group and individual images and their interrelations can an environment be constructed that will be satisfying to all. Until such knowledge is at hand, the designer must continue to rely upon the common denominator, or public image, and otherwise provide as great a variety of types of image-building material as he can devise.

The present studies have been confined to images as they exist at one point of time. We would understand them far better if we knew how they develop: how does a stranger build an image of a new city; how does a child develop his image of the world? How can such images be taught or communicated; what forms are most suitable for image development? A city must have both an obvious structure that can be grasped immediately and also a potential structure which will allow one gradually to construct a more complex and comprehensive picture.

The constant rebuilding of the city causes an allied problem: the adjustment of the image to external change. As our habitat becomes ever more fluid and shifting, it becomes critical to know how to maintain image continuity through these upheavals. How does an image adjust to change, and what are the limits within which this is possible? When is reality ignored or distorted to preserve the map? When does the image break down, and at what cost? How can this breakdown be avoided by physical continuities, or how can the formation of new images be facilitated, once breakdown has occurred? The construction of environmental images which are open-ended to change is a special problem: images which are tough and yet elastic in the face of the inevitable stresses.

This refers us again to the fact that the image is not solely the result of external characteristics but is a product of the observer as well. Therefore it would be possible to improve image quality by education. A useful study could be conducted on the devices by which one can teach people to be well oriented to their city environment: through museums, lectures, city walks, school projects, and so on. Allied with this is the potential use of symbolic devices: maps, signs, diagrams, direction-giving machines. A seemingly disordered physical world may be clarified by the invention of a symbolic diagram which explains the relations of main features in a way which is sympathetic to image development. A good example of this is the diagrammatic map of the London subway system, which is prominently displayed in every station.

Perhaps the most important direction for future study has been noted several times above: the lack of understanding of the city image as a total field, of the interrelations of elements, patterns, and sequences. City perception is in essence a time phenomenon, and it is directed toward an object of very large scale. If the environment is to be perceived as an organic whole, then the clarification of parts in their immediate context is only an elementary step. It will be extremely important to find ways of understanding and manipulating wholes, or at least of handling the problems of sequence and unfolding pattern.

It may turn out that some of these studies can in some way be quantified—be analyzed, for example, as to the number of bits of information needed to specify major city destinations, or as to relative redundancy. Speed of identification might be investigated, or the redundancy desirable for a sense of security, or the number of bits which a person can retain in regard to his environment. This ties back into the possibility of symbolic devices or direction-giving machines noted above.

But it seems likely that the core of the work will escape quantities, at least for some time, and that pattern and sequence considerations will be a primary direction. Involved in the latter is the technique of representation of complex, temporally extended patterns. Although this is a technical consideration, yet it is basic and difficult. Before such patterns can be understood or manipulated, ways must be found of representing their essence in such a way that they can be communicated without a repetition of the original experience. This is a rather baffling problem.

Since our original interest in the problem was as manipulators of the physical habitat, the trial use of these ideas in real design problems would also be high on the list of future studies. The design potential of imageability should be opened up, and the assertion that it could form the basis for a city design plan should be tested.

At the moment the most significant topics for future study appear to be these: the application of the concept to metropolitan regions; its extension to a consideration of major group differences; image development and adjustment to change; the city image as a total, temporally extended pattern; and the design potential of the concept of imageability.

C.

TWO EXAMPLES OF ANALYSIS

Figure 49

As examples of the type of detailed visual analysis of urban elements that can be made in the field, and of how this analysis can be related to interview results, we shall describe two adjacent localities in Boston: the highly identifiable district of Beacon Hill, and the confusing node of Scollay Square, which lies below it. Figure 49 shows the strategic position of these two elements in central Boston, and their relation to the West End, the downtown shopping district, the Common, and the Charles River.

Beacon Hill

Figure 50

One of the last of the original hills of the city, Beacon Hill lies between the commercial center and the river, thwarting the north-south flow of traffic, and visible from many points. The detail map shows the street pattern and the building coverage. This is a unique place, especially in an American city, a well-preserved relic of the early nineteenth century, still live and useful; a quiet, intimate upper-class residential area immediately adjacent to the very heart of the metropolis. In the interviews, it gave rise to a correspondingly strong image:

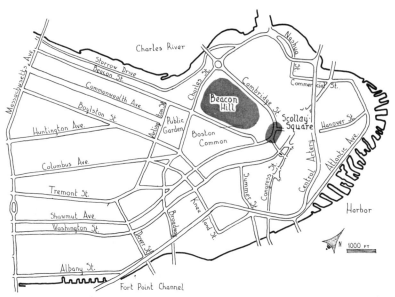

FIG. 49. *Location of Beacon Hill and Scollay Square in the Boston peninsula*

FIG. 50. *Streets and buildings, Beacon Hill*

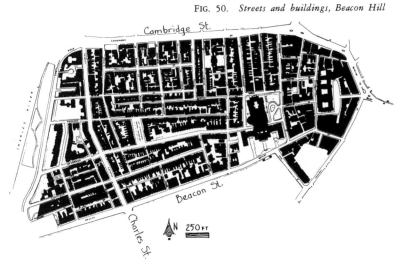

Beacon Hill was considered to be very distinctive, often felt to be the symbol of Boston, and often seen as from a distance. It was known to be in the center of the city, close to downtown, bounded sharply by Beacon Street and thus touching the Common. Conventionally, Cambridge Street divided it from the West End, and for most subjects, it stopped at Charles Street, although some hesitantly included the lower area. Nearly everyone was conscious of the connection to the river. The fourth edge was uncertain, usually at Joy Street or Bowdoin Street, but this is a confused area that "somehow" gets down to Scollay Square.

Internally, it seemed to have two distinct parts, a "back" and a "front" side, divided socially and visually along Myrtle Street. The street system was imaged as fairly parallel, "neat" or straight, but not well knit, and hard to get through. The front side was thought of as several parallel streets (Mt. Vernon Street being the most frequently named), with Louisburg Square at one end, and the State House at the other. The back side goes down to Cambridge Street. Joy Street seemed very important as the cross-connector. Beacon and Charles Streets were felt to be part of the whole, but Cambridge Street was not.

More than half the subjects expressed the following as part of their image of the Hill (in roughly descending order):

a sharp hill
narrow, pitching streets
the State House
Louisburg Square and its park
trees
handsome old houses
red brick
inset doorways

There were other frequent mentions of:

brick sidewalks
cobblestone streets
views of the river
a residential area
dirt and trash
social distinctions
corner stores on the back side
blocked or "curving" streets
the fence and statues, Louisburg Square
varied roof tops
signs on Charles Street

the gold dome of the State House
purple windows
some apartment houses in contrast

Still other comments are added by at least three people:

parked cars
bay windows
ironwork
houses packed together
old street lamps
a "European" flavor
the Charles River
the view to the Massachusetts General Hospital
children at play on the back side
black shutters
antique shops on Charles Street
three- and four-story houses

The hurried, casual situation of asking directions in the street produced a surprising number of comments. Essentially they included: it is a hill, and one goes up streets or up stairs to get to it. It is marked by the State House, which has a gold dome and stairs. It borders on the Common, with Beacon Street as an edge, and contains Louisburg Square, which has a park and a fence. Several additions were made by two or more people: it has trees; it is high-class residence; it is near Scollay Square; it contains Joy, Grove, and Charles Streets. These comments, in their abbreviated fashion, echoed the results of the more intensive interviews.

Let us look at the physical reality underlying these themes which appeared in the image of the Hill. The district does indeed coincide very closely with a sharp, unique hill, whose steepest slopes lie toward Charles and Cambridge Streets. The slope continues past Cambridge into the West End somewhat, but in fact the steep gradient, the point of inflection of the vertical curve, is already past, and this inflection seems to be the visually significant event. The edge of the slope lies very precisely at Charles Street, and this makes incorporation of the lower area into Beacon Hill difficult, as we shall see later. On the other two sides, however, the boundaries have encroached up the sides of the Hill. Beacon Street is part-way up the slopes, and the Common is substantially part of the same topographic feature. Yet the change in space and character is strong enough to override this topographic blurring, and "Beacon Hill" begins clearly at Beacon Street, even if the geographic hill begins at Tremont.

Figure 51, page 164

On the east, however, the situation differs. Here a substantial part of the hill has been overbuilt with commercial uses, so that Scollay Square is on the side-hill, and School Street has a steep up-gradient. The topographic reality has been ignored, and yet there is no large spatial opening which will make visible what has been done, nor a strong character change which can override the continuity of the land form. This undoubtedly contributes to the fuzziness of the image on this side, as well as to the spatial uneasiness of Scollay Square.

Within the Hill, the sense of gradient is ever-present, visually and in terms of physical effort and balance. The fact that the street slopes are predominantly in two different directions on the front and back sides tends to emphasize the distinction of these areas.

The spatial quality of development on the front side of the Hill is unmistakable. It consists of continuous street corridors, everywhere of an intimate scale. Building façades are close at hand, and often of three stories, giving the feeling that these row dwellings are all single-family structures. Apartments, rooming houses, and institutions are not easily distinguishable. Within these limits of character, however, there are significant variations of proportion, as shown in the diagrammatic cross sections. In particular, there is a substantial change on Mt. Vernon Street above Louisburg Square,

Figure 51

Figure 52

FIG. 51. *Steep streets, topography, and street cross sections*

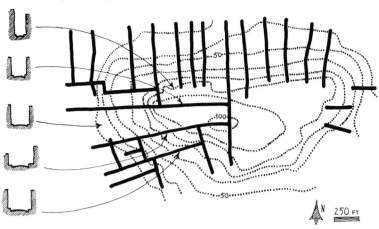

FIG. 52. *Looking up Chestnut Street from Charles Street*

where a long row of "great" houses is set back on the north side, allowing small front yards to appear. This is a very noticeable and pleasant change, which does not break the continuity of the whole.

The proportions of the space change very noticeably on the back side; the structures become four to six stories high, obviously not single-family affairs. The corridor space becomes canyon-like. Since the slope is here toward the north, the sunlight touches the streets more rarely. These sensations of spatial proportions, of light, of gradient, and of social connotation appear to be the primary characteristics of the area.

Figures 53 and 54 show the location on the Hill of other thematic elements which seem to identify the image. It may be remarked again that these are primarily the characteristics of the front side. The distribution of brick sidewalks, of corner stores, of inset doorways, of ornamental ironwork, of trees, to some extent of black shutters, all hammer home the uniqueness of the front side and of its distinction from the back. The concentration and repetition of such themes, and the level of maintenance evidenced in polished brass, fresh paint, clean pavements, and well-furnished windows,

Figures 53 and 54, page 166

165

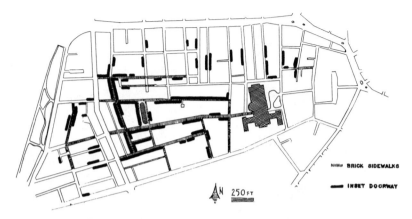

FIG. 53. *Inset doorways and brick sidewalks*

have a strong cumulative effect, which adds a certain vitality to the image of the Hill.

Figure 55, page 167
Bay windows are less characteristic, except along one piece of lower Pinckney Street, and the purple windows, popularly associated with the Hill, in reality rarely appear. The same is true of cobblestone pavements, which actually are visible only in two short, narrow

FIG. 54. *Bow fronts and ornamental ironwork*

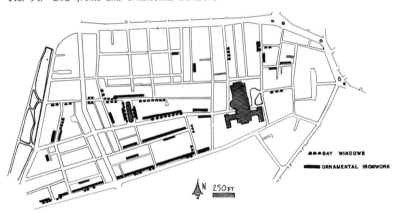

strips at Louisburg Square, and along obscure Acorn Street. Brick is indeed the almost universal building material, and, although this is hardly distinctive in Boston, it sets a consistent background of color and texture. The old street lamps also appear throughout the area.

The visual sub-areas on the Hill are each rather clearly delineated by visual characteristics of space, gradient, use, floor, vegetation, and such details as doors, shutters, and ironwork. Normally these characters occur together, reinforcing the distinction. Thus the front side is an area of steep gradient to Charles Street; of intimately scaled street corridors; of ornamented, highly maintained structures saying upper-class; of sunlight, street trees, and flowers, brick side-walks, black shutters, and inset doorways; of maids, chauffeurs, old ladies, and fine cars on the streets. The back side grades down to Cambridge Street, with darker canyon spaces bordered by bare, poorly maintained tenement structures, dotted with corner stores, its streets dirty, its children playing on the pavements. Some stone

Figure 56, page 169

FIG. 55. *The thematic unit of Beacon Hill*

structures appear among the brick ones. Trees now appear in back courtyards, rather than in the street.

Lower Beacon Hill, between Charles Street and the Charles River, shares many characteristics with the front side: vegetation, brick and brick walks, inset doors, and ornamental iron, but the lack of gradient and the barrier of Charles Street seem to place it in a classificatory limbo. Charles Street itself is a sub-area in its own right, being a shopping street with a special character due to the rather expensive or nostalgic types of goods sold there, which are consumed higher up the Hill. The distribution of antique shops illustrates this point. The governmental area, introduced by the massive break of the State House, is completely different in use, spatial scale, and street activity. There remains the transition zone between Hancock and Somerset Streets, below Deane Street, which has examples of the Beacon Hill characters: slope, brick walks, bay windows, inset doors, and ornamental iron. But it is cut off; it has stores and churches mixed with the residential use; and its maintenance speaks of a social class below that of the front side itself. This lack of definite demarcation is further cause for the difficulty in imagining the shape of the Hill on this side.

It is interesting to see the effect of the circulation channels, or lack of them. The obstacles presented to moving from the front to the back side, as well as the fact that the normal approach to these two sides is from different directions, serves to isolate one from another. The State House cuts off Bowdoin Street from the residential area, except for the rather cluttered passage under the arch, which has a most unpromising approach from the east. To an even greater extent, the difficulty in moving down to Scollay Square makes the Square "float" with reference to the Hill.

On the other hand, the through streets take on added importance: Mt. Vernon, Joy, Bowdoin, and Charles. All streets, although topologically regular, and although those named above in fact go through, are visually blocked, which reinforces the compactness, intimacy, and identity of the area. Joy, Bowdoin, and Pinckney Streets are blocked by vertical curves; Mt. Vernon, Cedar, and Charles Streets by slight horizontal bends. All the others dead end in the region. Thus it is impossible to see through at any point.

Nevertheless, there are some fine views out from the Hill, particularly those of the Charles River, down Chestnut, Mt. Vernon, Pinckney, Myrtle, and Revere Streets, which are produced by the slope of these streets and the Hill's enfilade position on the river. There is a pleasant glimpse of the Common, from Mt. Vernon down

Figure 57

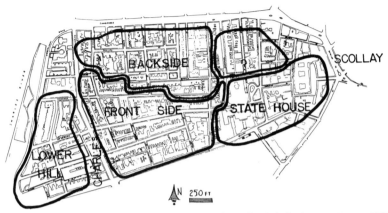

FIG. 56. Sub-districts on Beacon Hill

FIG. 56. *Sub-districts on Beacon Hill*

Walnut Street. All the north-running "back-side" streets look out over the West End, but the view of roof tops is hardly remarkable, except for the sight of the original Bulfinch hospital down Anderson Street (which is also the only back-to-front connection between Cedar and Joy Streets). Coming up Pinckney Street there is a startling view of a decapitated Custom House Tower, while up

FIG. 57. *Landmarks and commercial uses*

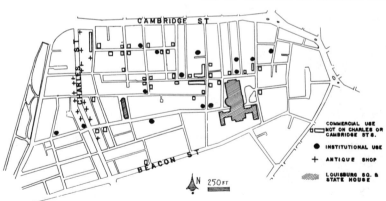

169

Chestnut Street one gets a very handsome sight of the State House gold dome.

Figure 58

The State House, of course, is the primary landmark on the Hill. Its unique shape and function, as well as its location close to the crest of the Hill and its visual exposure to the Common, make it a key for central Boston as a whole. It acts both within and with-

Figure 59

out the Hill. Louisburg Square is the other basic locality, being a small residential node on the lower slopes of the front side. It is neither visually exposed, nor fixed with relation to hill crest or foot, nor anchored by any other device. Thus it is not used as a locator, but is rather thought of as being "somewhere inside" the Hill, and the very epitome of its particular character. It may be noted, indeed, how the front-side themes are all concentrated here, appear as it were in their purest form. In addition, the Square is a formed space, which contrasts with and yet expresses more clearly the spatial character of the area. It contains the famous tiny areas of cobblestones, and a fenced and intensely green park, furnished with statues, which compels attention both by its lushness and its implied "no trespassing." It is interesting that the side-hill character

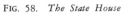

FIG. 58. *The State House*

of the Square, although it makes firm location difficult in the total structure, does not seem to disturb the visual stability of the immediate space.

There are a few other landmarks of some importance in the internal structure. These include: the Universalist Church on Mt. Vernon and Charles Streets, which is remarkable both for its position and its spire; the Suffolk Law School, facing the State House on Deane Street, which adds its bulk to the character and boundary of the governmental district; the New England College of Pharmacy, which intrudes on the residential character of Mt. Vernon Street; and the Carnegie Institute, on Pinckney Street at Anderson Street, which breaks the continuous housing façades and marks the entrance to the back side. There are other non-residential uses on the Hill, but they fade into the general background surprisingly well. Very few landmarks, external to the Hill, are visible within it, and thus its internal structure is thrown upon its own resources.

Figure 57, page 169

The connection of the Hill to the West End via a sharp boundary, and the confusion of the transition to Scollay Square, have already been discussed. That the Hill fronts on the Common is clear to

FIG. 59. *Louisburg Square*

all, but it should be added that the direct linkage between the two is quite weak. Easy passage from one to the other is blocked except at Charles, Joy, and Walnut Streets, and the view of the massed green trees is equally lacking. The planting on the Hill thus lacks the continuity it might have had with the park, if paths or openings had existed perpendicular to the line of Beacon Street.

Some relation to the Charles River was sensed by almost everyone, probably because of the fine views down the east-west streets, but the detailed linkage was quite unclear, because of the dubious classification of the lower area, the flattened foreshore, and the difficulty of crossing Storrow Drive to reach the water. The relationship with the river, which is apparent on the slopes above, seems to disappear as one approaches it.

In the wider context of the entire city, Beacon Hill has an important role to play, despite the restricted number of its inhabitants. By its topography, street spaces, trees, social class, detail, and level of maintenance, it is differentiated from any other area in Boston. The region most nearly similar is Back Bay, with a continuity in material, vegetation, association, and to some extent use and status; but with a dissimilar topography, detail, and maintenance. Confusion between the two occurred at times, however. The only other possible similarity would be with Copps Hill in the North End: also on a hill, old, and residential, but differing sharply in class, space, detail, lack of trees, and absence of boundaries.

This unique area, therefore, stands out over the city center, linking Back Bay, Common, downtown, and the West End; and in potential dominating and focusing the entire central region. Potentially again, it could explain and fix the direction change in the Charles River bank, otherwise difficult to recall, yet vital in the total city structure. When viewing Boston from Cambridge, the Hill plays an important role, not only in enlivening, but in explaining and articulating the sequence of parts appearing in the panorama: Back Bay—Beacon Hill—West End. From other parts of they city, however, except the West End and the Common, the Hill is not visible as an entity, because of its gradual ascent and the intervening obstacles. As a traffic obstacle, it guides the flows around its base, and concentrates attention on the encircling paths and nodes: Charles Street, Cambridge Street, Scollay Square.

The Hill thus proves to be a region whose physical characteristics back up the strength of the popular image, and which contains many illustrations of the psychological effects of the disposing of paths, slopes, spaces, boundaries, and the concentration of detail. It also appears, despite its strength, to fall somewhat short of its potential as a dominant hill, particularly because of its internal divisions, the flaws in its relation to the Charles River, the Boston Common, and Scollay Square, and the lack of exploitation of its visual eminence over the city, particularly through outward views. The power and satisfaction of this particular urban image, however—its continuity, humanity, and delight—are unmistakable.

Scollay Square

Scollay Square is quite another story, being a node which is structurally vital but which did not seem easy to identify or describe. Its location in Boston, and role as a strategic traffic interchange, may be seen by reference again to Figure 49. Figure 60 is a more detailed map of the Square, illustrating its principal physical features.

Figures 49 and 60, pages 161 and 175

The public image of Scollay Square was that of an important junction node for paths going around Beacon Hill and between the central area and the North End. Into it came Cambridge Street, Tremont Street, Court Street (or was it State Street?), and a series of streets leading to Dock Square, Faneuil Hall, Haymarket Square, and the North End. Hanover Street used to make a clear path to the North End, but it is now blocked and this was confusing. Scollay Square was sometimes extended to include Bowdoin Square, sometimes not.

The Pemberton Square entrance was not generally remembered, except by old hands. Cambridge Street, however, made a clear joint with Scollay Square, and its curve was vivid. Tremont Street was known to go in, but the entrance was neither remarkable nor always certain. Washington Street was thought by many subjects to run into the Square, and confusion was common as between Tremont Street, Court Street, and the imagined presence of Washington or State Streets. Except for the blocked-off Hanover Street, the streets going to Dock Square, North End, or Haymarket Square were not individually known or differentiated. As a group, they seemed to run off downhill, curving as they went. Most important were the general level relations: Beacon Hill was above; Scollay Square was a sloping hillside plateau; Cambridge and Tremont Streets followed around the contours; the other streets went away downhill.

The Square was shapeless, hard to visualize, "just another crossing of streets," although the Bowdoin Square end was somewhat differentiated from the rest. The main feature was the central subway entrance. There was a pervasive, recognizable tone of dilapidation, marginal use, and "low-class" amusement.

More than half of the persons interviewed agreed on the following:

Cambridge Street runs into it, curving and tapering as it does so.
The Square sits halfway up a hill and streets run up or down to it.

More than a quarter added:

Tremont Street runs into it.
There is a subway entrance in the middle.
Hanover Street goes into it.
Court Street runs off of it, curving downhill (or is it State Street?).

At least three could say:

Streets go down to Dock Square and Faneuil Hall.
There are barrooms there.
There is some confused relation to Washington Street.

The street inquiries elicited only the following frequently repeated comments:

It's on the subway line.
Tremont Street goes into it.

While two to four people stopped in the streets could add these thoughts:

Cambridge Street runs into it.
Washington Street runs into it (incorrect).
There's a subway island in the middle.
Streets run up or down to it.
Streets from the North End go to it, beyond and under the Artery.
Movie theaters.
A "Boston square," just a street crossing.
A "big" square, a "big place."
A garage at one end.

Clearly, the comments were scanty in comparison to those about Beacon Hill, except for the enumeration of the connecting paths, and these are abstractly described and often confused. Yet Scollay Square plays a key structural role in Boston, visually gray as it may be.

The real Scollay Square is in plan a rather orderly space, the square proper (from Sudbury to Court Streets) being a long rectangle, with small entering streets at irregular intervals. In plan, the path system has some reasonableness, being a simple spindle shape, with three additional filaments on one side and two on the other. In three dimensions, however, this order is not apparent:

Figure 60

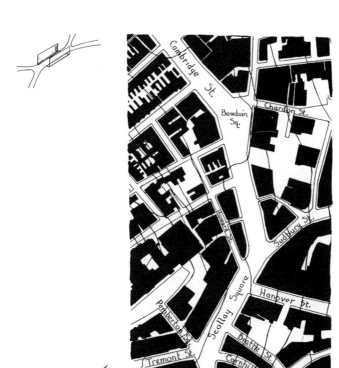

FIG. 60. *Streets and buildings, Scollay Square*

gap-toothed sides and the mass of traffic shred the space, and the cross-slanted floor is also disturbing. If anything tends to rescue one's sense of stability, it is the large billboard facing the Square from the corner of Sudbury and Cambridge Streets, a gaudy advertisement which ends the space firmly, if not handsomely.

Figure 61, page 177

The path form is obscured because one of the spindle arms, Sudbury Street, has the look of a relatively minor street, and many of the path entrances are difficult to distinguish. The sense of side-hill pervades the area and its approaches, and, while destructive of the sense of spatial stability, it is the principal key to relations with areas out of sight.

The space continues to the northwest, leaking out via the broad Cambridge Street to Bowdoin Square, which is more properly an intersection, an inflection of Cambridge Street itself. Between Bowdoin and Scollay Squares, the space is utterly shapeless and uncontrolled, to a degree that makes maintenance of direction precarious, except for the clue furnished by the flow of traffic. Traffic is indeed a dominant impression of the area. The Square is continually full of cars, and the lines of heavy flow become the key paths, regardless of other visual characteristics.

Within the Square, there is little in the physical structures that would give any sense of homogeneity or character. The structures are of many shapes and sizes, of mixed materials, both old and relatively new. The common feature is simply a prevailing look of dilapidation. The uses and activities in the lower stories, however, have more consistency. On both sides of the Square there is a continuous string of bars, cheap restaurants, amusement arcades, movie theaters, cut-rate services, and stores selling second-hand goods or novelties, a string unbroken except for some empty stores on the west side. Associated with these uses are both the physical details of store front and signs, and the character of the people on the walks, where the homeless, the alcoholic, and the shore-leave sailor leaven the usual downtown crowds. At night Scollay Square becomes more distinguishable from the bulk of central Boston, since its lights, activities, and sidewalk population are in sharp contrast to the dark and quiet city.

The principal visual impressions 'of Scollay Square, therefore, are spatial shapelessness, heavy traffic, sharp slopes, and a homogeneity of dilapidation', particular uses, and characteristic inhabitants. Most of these characteristics are not so unusual in the city that Scollay Square should become an unmistakable place. The dilapidation and many of the uses are common to numerous locations marginal to the downtown area, and the special combination of use and inhabitant is repeated, in an even stronger way, along Washington Street between Dover Street and Broadway. Spatial chaos at a multiple intersection of paths is a frequent event in Boston, and other examples, such as Bowdoin Square, Dock Square, Park Square, Church Green, or Harrison and Essex Streets, are easy to find. The long rectangular plan of Scollay may be unique, but it is not visually apparent. The slope of this node, as well as its structural relationship to Boston as a whole, is undoubtedly its primary identification feature.

Since Scollay Square plays its most important role as a junction of paths, it is important to see it, not statically, but as it reveals itself on approach, and how one leaves it behind. The approach from Tremont Street, which dips slightly into it, reveals the node as a lowering of the building mass, the obvious edge of the central business district, with a first view of an old brick building and sign on the corner of Cornhill, and then an unraveling of space and weather-beaten signs to the left. There is a striking impression of massed cars.

Washington Street leads primarily to Dock Square, and Court Street, which is the connection to Scollay, appears to be only a minor and undistinguished cross street, although the corner is marked by the Old State House. Court Street itself leads in a rather sidelong and mincing manner up to Scollay Square.

Cambridge Street goes southeast rather convincingly toward the goal of the big and distinctive, if faceless, Telephone Building at

FIG. 61. *Scollay Square looking north*

Bowdoin Square. Here, however, the path bears right into spatial chaos, and all sense of goal or direction is lost. Only a further right swing at Sudbury Street makes apparent the characteristic configuration of bars, tall office buildings behind, and subway station in the center.

The downhill streets—Sudbury, Hanover, Brattle, and Cornhill— all pick up a marked slope as they approach the Square. On each, there is some sense of opening ahead, and perhaps of a thickening of bars and other associated uses, but generally the Square itself is far less perceptible in advance than is the County Courthouse Annex on Pemberton Square, which towers on the skyline. Scollay Square seems to be simply an end, or a twist, in the street. The upward curve of Cornhill is a pleasant spatial experience in itself (as it was designed to be), but the arrival at Scollay Square is without interest. From the uphill side as well, on Pemberton Square and Howard Street, the Square is indistinguishable. Thus only Cambridge Street, despite the confusion beyond Bowdoin Street, has an approach with some quality of identifiability.

The direction out on Cambridge Street is also relatively clear, while the once important Hanover Street is now hard to distinguish from the rest, except for some extra width. Sudbury Street as well, which now carries appreciable traffic, seems by its size and bordering use to be a very minor street. As seen from the north, the entrance to the important Tremont Street is sharply turned and almost invisible. Many interviewees had difficulty locating this exit, but once it is found, the direction on Tremont Street is quite clear, with the sequential appearance of such clues as the Beacon Hill Theater, the Parker House, King's Chapel, the Tremont Temple, the Granary Burying-Ground, and the Common.

The space of the Square leads very strongly downhill and slightly left through Court Street, although the automobile traffic contradicts this impression by being one-way up into the Square at this point. If one continues to walk down Court Street, there is no clue to the presence of Washington Street, and one is aware only of the Old State House and a confused space. The relation of Washington Street to Scollay Square is thus obscured in both directions.

It is further confusing that Court Street and Cornhill enter the Square so closely together, and yet a block away have destinations which seem psychologically as far apart as State Street and Dock Square. Again we conclude that in outward movement the Cambridge Street path is the only clearly identifiable one, although the trouble at Tremont Street is rather brief.

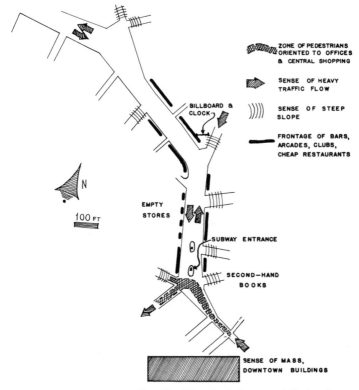

FIG. 62. *The visual elements of Scollay Square*

The Square gains some connection with the exterior, other than by slopes or paths, by means of outward views. These include the Telephone Building at Bowdoin Square and the Courthouse Annex on Pemberton Square (which are architecturally almost indistinguishable except for their differences in height), and the highly identifiable Custom House Tower, visible to the southeast as the mark of the lower end of State Street and the waterfront. Most striking of all is the mass of office buildings visible on the skyline to the south, which indicates the Post Office Square district, and which makes clear Scollay Square's marginal position at the fringe of the downtown core.

Unlike Beacon Hill or Commonwealth Avenue, Scollay Square is essentially invisible from the outside, except immediately on approach. Only the old hand would remember on noting the Courthouse Annex from a distance that it is fairly close to Scollay Square.

Figure 62, page 179

Internally, there is relatively little to differentiate directions or parts of the Square. The principal internal landmark is the subway entrance and newsstand, which cling to a tiny oval in the midst of the traffic. Yet even this is low and hard to distinguish from a distance. It is primarily apparent as a yellow-lettered sign, and a hole in the ground. Its impact is reduced by the presence of a similar structure on a similar oval just behind it. This second doorway to the underground, however, is an exit only, with few uses and no newsstand, and thus perceptually "dead." The subway entrance, which seems to everyone to be "in the middle of" Scollay Square, is actually almost at the very end. One other striking detail in the Square is the brightly lettered tobacco shop on the corner of Pemberton and Tremont Streets, which lies at the foot of, and in sharp contrast to, the sheer wall of the Suffolk Bank.

There are few direction clues inside the Square, except for the sideward slant and the dominant lines of traffic, which confer an axial sense. There is no appreciable gradient in the space or the massing of buildings. The tall buildings on the skyline to the south and the terminal billboard to the north are the principal differentiations of direction in the setting itself.

There are substantial signals of direction in the variety of use and activity, however. The density of pedestrians and turning traffic is highest on the southern end, where there are uses of the type normally servicing the downtown business center: drugstores, restaurants, and tobacconists. Here the pedestrian stream is the usual mixture of office workers and shoppers. The cheap goods stores tend to collect more on the east than the west side of the Square, while the flop houses and rooming hotels lie to the west, penetrating upward toward the fringes of the Beacon Hill transition area. The pedestrians here are those popularly associated with the Square. The cluster of second-hand book stores on Cornhill is another internal clue. The northern fringes of the area run off to lofts and warehousing. Thus, while physically inchoate, Scollay Square is internally differentiated and structured by the slopes, the traffic, and the pattern of uses.

The Square, therefore, needs visual identity to match its functional importance, a realization of such potential forms as the rectangular space, the spindle pattern of paths, the side-hill terracing. To fulfill its structural role, the joint of each important path must be clearly explained, both inbound and outbound. Potentially it could play an even more striking visual role as the central point of the old head of the Boston peninsula, the hub of a whole series of districts (Beacon Hill, West End, North End, market area, financial district, central shopping district), the node of such important paths as Tremont, Cambridge, Court-State, and Sudbury Streets; and as the central figure in the descending triad of nodal terraces: Pemberton, Scollay, and Dock Squares. Scollay Square is not only a locus of uses which make "nice" people uneasy—it is also a great visual opportunity missed.

BIBLIOGRAPHY

1. Angyal, A., "Über die Raumlage vorgestellter Oerter," *Archiv für die Gesamte Psychologie*, Vol. 78, 1930, pp. 47–94.
2. Automotive Safety Foundation, *Driver Needs in Freeway Signing*, Washington, Dec. 1958.
3. Bell, Sir Charles, *The People of Tibet*, Oxford, Clarendon Press, 1928.
4. Best, Elsdon, *The Maori*, Wellington, H. H. Tombs, 1924.
5. Binet, M. A., "Reverse Illusions of Orientation," *Psychological Review*, Vol. I, No. 4, July 1894, pp. 337–350.
6. Bogoraz-Tan, Vladimir Germanovich, "The Chukchee," *Memoirs of the American Museum of Natural History*, Vol. XI, Leiden, E. J. Brill; and New York, G. E. Stechert, 1904, 1907, 1909.
7. Boulding, Kenneth E., *The Image*, Ann Arbor, University of Michigan Press, 1956.
8. Brown, Warner, "Spatial Integrations in a Human Maze," *University of California Publications in Psychology*, Vol. V, No. 5, 1932, pp. 123–134.
9. Carpenter, Edmund, "Space Concepts of the Aivilik Eskimos," *Explorations*, Vol. V, p. 134.
10. Casamajor, Jean, "Le Mystérieux Sens de l'Espace," *Revue Scientifique*, Vol. 65, No. 18, 1927, pp. 554–565.
11. Casamorata, Cesare, "I Canti di Firenze," *L'Universo*, Marzo-Aprile, 1944, Anno XXV, Number 3.

12. Claparède, Edouard, "L'Orientation Lointaine," *Nouveau Traité de Psychologie*, Tome VIII, Fasc. 3, Paris, Presses Universitaires de France, 1943.

13. Cornetz, V., "Le Cas Elémentaire du Sens de la Direction chez l'Homme," *Bulletin de la Société de Géographie d'Alger*, 18e Année, 1913, p. 742.

14. Cornetz, V., "Observation sur le Sens de la Direction chez l'Homme," *Revue des Idées*, 15 Juillet, 1909.

15. Colucci, Cesare, "Sui disturbi dell'orientamento topografico," *Annali di Nevrologia*, Vol. XX, Anno X, 1902, pp. 555–596.

16. Donaldson, Bess Allen, *The Wild Rue: A Study of Muhammadan Magic and Folklore in Iran*, London, Lirzac, 1938.

17. Elliott, Henry Wood, *Our Arctic Province*, New York, Scribners, 1886.

18. Finsch, Otto, "Ethnologische erfahrungen und belegstücke aus der Südsee," Vienna, Naturhistorisches Hofmuseum, *Annalen*. Vol. 3, 1888, pp. 83–160, 293–364. Vol. 6, 1891, pp. 13–36, 37–130. Vol. 8, 1893, pp. 1–106, 119–275, 295–437.

19. Firth, Raymond, *We, the Tikopia*, London, Allen and Unwin Ltd., 1936.

20. Fischer, M. H., "Die Orientierung im Raume bei Wirbeltieren und beim Menschen," in *Handbuch der Normalen und Pathologischen Physiologie*, Berlin, J. Springer, 1931, pp. 909–1022.

21. Flanagan, Thomas, "Amid the Wild Lights and Shadows," *Columbia University Forum*, Winter 1957.

22. Forster, E. M., *A Passage to India*, New York, Harcourt, 1949.

23. Gatty, Harold, *Nature Is Your Guide*, New York, E. P. Dutton, 1958.

24. Gautier, Emile Félix, *Missions au Sahara*, Paris, Librairie A. Colin, 1908.

25. Gay, John, *Trivia, or, The Art of Walking the Streets of London*, Introd. and notes by W. H. Williams, London, D. O'Connor, 1922.

26. Geoghegan, Richard Henry, *The Aleut Language*, Washington, U. S. Department of Interior, 1944.

27. Gemelli, Agostino, Tessier, G., and Galli, A., "La Percezione della Posizione del nostro corpo e dei suoi spostamenti," *Archivio Italiano di Psicologia*, I, 1920, pp. 104–182.

28. Gemelli, Agostino, "L'Orientazione Lontana nel Volo in Aeroplano," *Rivista Di Psicologia*, Anno 29, No. 4, Oct.–Dec. 1933, p. 297.

29. Gennep, A. Van, "Du Sens d'Orientation chez l'Homme," *Réligions, Moeurs, et Légendes*, 3e Séries, Paris, 1911, p. 47.

30. Granpré-Molière, M. J., "Landscape of the N. E. Polder," translated from *Forum*, Vol. 10:1–2, 1955.

31. Griffin, Donald R., "Sensory Physiology and the Orientation of Animals," *American Scientist,* April 1953, pp. 209–244.

32. de Groot, J. J. M., *Religion in China,* New York, G. P. Putnam's, 1912.

33. Gill, Eric, *Autobiography,* New York City, Devin-Adair, 1941.

34. Halbwachs, Maurice, *La Mémoire Collective,* Paris, Presses Universitaires de France, 1950.

35. Homo, Leon, *Rome Impériale et l'Urbanisme dans l'Antiquité,* Paris, Michel, 1951.

36. Jaccard, Pierre, "Une Enquête sur la Désorientation en Montagne," *Bulletin de la Société Vaudoise des Science Naturelles,* Vol. 56, No. 217, August 1926, pp. 151–159.

37. Jaccard, Pierre, *Le Sens de la Direction et L'Orientation Lointaine chez l'Homme,* Paris, Payot, 1932.

38. Jackson, J. B., "Other-Directed Houses," *Landscape,* Winter, 1956–57, Vol. 6, No. 2.

39. Kawaguchi, Ekai, *Three Years in Tibet,* Adyar, Madras, The Theosophist Office, 1909.

40. Kepes, Gyorgy, *The New Landscape,* Chicago, P. Theobald, 1956.

41. Kilpatrick, Franklin P., "Recent Experiments in Perception," *New York Academy of Sciences, Transactions,* No. 8, Vol. 16. June 1954, pp. 420–425.

42. Langer, Suzanne, *Feeling and Form: A Theory of Art,* New York, Scribner, 1953.

43. Lewis, C. S., "The Shoddy Lands," in *The Best from Fantasy and Science Fiction,* New York, Doubleday, 1957.

44. Lyons, Henry, "The Sailing Charts of the Marshall Islanders," *Geographical Journal,* Vol. LXXII, No. 4, October 1928, pp. 325–328.

45. Maegraith, Brian G., "The Astronomy of the Aranda and Luritja Tribes," Adelaide University Field Anthropology, Central Australia no. 10, taken from *Transactions of the Royal Society of South Australia,* Vol. LVI, 1932.

46. Malinowski, Bronislaw, *Argonauts of the Western Pacific,* London, Routledge, 1922.

47. Marie, Pierre, et Behague, P., "Syndrome de Désorientation dans l'Espace" *Revue Neurologique,* Vol. 26, No. 1, 1919, pp. 1–14.

48. Morris, Charles W., *Foundations of the Theory of Signs,* Chicago, University of Chicago Press, 1938.

49. *New York Times,* April 30, 1957, article on the "Directomat."

50. Nice, M., "Territory in Bird Life," *American Midland Naturalist,* Vol. 26, pp. 441–487.

51. Paterson, Andrew and Zangwill, O. L., "A Case of Topographic Disorientation," *Brain,* Vol. LXVIII, Part 3, September 1945, pp. 188–212.

52. Peterson, Joseph, "Illusions of Direction Orientation," *Journal of Philosophy, Psychology and Scientific Methods,* Vol. XIII, No. 9, April 27, 1916, pp. 225–236.

53. .Pink, Olive M., "The Landowners in the Northern Division of the Aranda Tribe, Central Australia," *Oceania,* Vol. VI, No. 3, March 1936, pp. 275–305.

54. Pink, Olive M., "Spirit Ancestors in a Northern Aranda Horde Country," *Oceania,* Vol. IV, No. 2, December 1933, pp. 176–186.

55. Porteus, S. D., *The Psychology of a Primitive People,* New York City, Longmans, Green, 1931.

56. Pratolini, Vasco, *Il Quartiere,* Firenze, Valleschi, 1947.

57. Proust, Marcel, *Du Côté de chez Swann,* Paris, Gallimand, 1954.

58. Proust, Marcel, *Albertine Disparue,* Paris, Nouvelle Revue Française, 1925.

59. Rabaud, Etienne, *L'Orientation Lointaine et la Reconnaissance des Lieux,* Paris, Alcan, 1927.

60. Rasmussen, Knud Johan Victor, *The Netsilik Eskimos* (Report of the Fifth Thule Expedition, 1921–24, Vol. 8, No. 1–2) Copenhagen, Gyldendal, 1931.

61. Rattray, R. S., *Religion and Art in Ashanti,* Oxford, Clarendon Press, 1927.

62. Reichard, Gladys Amanda, *Navaho Religion, a Study of Symbolism,* New York, Pantheon, 1950.

63. Ryan, T. A. and M. S., "Geographical Orientation," *American Journal of Psychology,* Vol. 53, 1940, pp. 204–215.

64. Sachs, Curt, *Rhythm and Tempo,* New York, Norton, 1953.

65. Sandström, Carl Ivan, *Orientation in the Present Space,* Stockholm, Almqvist and Wiksell, 1951.

66. Sapir, Edward, "Language and Environment," *American Anthropologist,* Vol. 14, 1912.

67. Sauer, Martin, *An Account of a Geographical and Astronomical Expedition to the Northern Parts of Russia,* London, T. Cadell, 1802.

68. Shen, Tsung-lien and Liu-Shen-chi, *Tibet and the Tibetans,* Stanford, Stanford University Press, 1953.

69. Shepard, P., "Dead Cities in the American West," *Landscape,* Winter, Vol. 6, No. 2, 1956–57.

70. Shipton, Eric Earle, *The Mount Everest Reconnaissance Expedition,* London, Hodder and Stoughton, 1952.

71. deSilva, H. R., "A Case of a Boy Possessing an Automatic Directional Orientation," *Science,* Vol. 73, No. 1893, April 10, 1931, pp. 393–394.

72. Spencer, Baldwin and Gillen, F. J., *The Native Tribes of Central Australia,* London, Macmillan, 1899.

73. Stefánsson, Vihljálmur, "The Stefánsson-Anderson Arctic Expedition of the American Museum: Preliminary Ethnological Report," *Anthropological Papers of the American Museum of Natural History,* Vol. XIV, Part 1, New York City, 1914.

74. Stern, Paul, "On the Problem of Artistic Form," *Logos,* Vol. V, 1914–15, pp. 165–172.

75. Strehlow, Carl, *Die Aranda und Loritza-stämme in Zentral Australien,* Frankfurt am Main, J. Baer, 1907–20.

76. Trowbridge, C. C., "On Fundamental Methods of Orientation and Imaginary Maps," *Science,* Vol. 38, No. 990, Dec. 9, 1913, pp. 888–897.

77. Twain, Mark, *Life on the Mississippi,* New York, Harper, 1917.

78. Waddell, L. Austine, *The Buddhism of Tibet or Lamaism,* London, W. H. Allen, 1895.

79. Whitehead, Alfred North, *Symbolism and Its Meaning and Effect,* New York, Macmillan, 1958.

80. Winfield, Gerald F., *China: The Land and the People,* New York, Wm. Sloane Association, 1948.

81. Witkin, H. A., "Orientation in Space," *Research Reviews,* Office of Naval Research, December 1949.

82. Wohl, R. Richard and Strauss, Anselm L., "Symbolic Representation and the Urban Milieu," *American Journal of Sociology,* Vol. LXIII, No. 5, March 1958, pp. 523–532.

83. Yung, Emile, "Le Sens de la Direction," *Echo des Alpes,* No. 4, 1918, p. 110.

* Italicized page numbers refer to illustrations.

190

Credits for Photographs